BALLYMACANDY

THE STORY OF A KERRY AMBUSH

Owen O'Shea, from Milltown, Co. Kerry, is a historian and author of several books on history and politics in his native county. A former press adviser to the Labour Party and a journalist for many years, he is the author of *Heirs to the Kingdom: Kerry's Political Dynasties* (2011) and co-author of *A Century of Politics in the Kingdom: A County Kerry Compendium* (Merrion Press, 2018). He was co-editor of a history of Kerry and the Easter Rising in 2016. O'Shea currently works as Media, Communications and Customer Relations Officer with Kerry County Council and is an Irish Research Council-funded PhD student at University College Dublin, researching electioneering and politics in Kerry in the decade after the Civil War.

BALLYMACANDY

THE STORY OF A KERRY AMBUSH

OWEN O'SHEA

MERRION
PRESS

First published in 2021 by
Merrion Press
10 George's Street
Newbridge
Co. Kildare
Ireland
www.merrionpress.ie

© Owen O'Shea, 2021

9781785373879 (Paper)
9781785373886 (Kindle)
9781785373893 (Epub)

A CIP catalogue record for this book is
available from the British Library.

Typeset in Minion Pro 11/16 pt

Front cover: Members of the Royal Irish Constabulary
at Milltown Barracks in 1914.

Back cover: Members of the Milltown Volunteers, *c.*1918.

Merrion Press is a member of Publishing Ireland.

CONTENTS

Foreword: Dr Mary McAuliffe   vii

Preface   1

Prologue – Salve Regina   5

 1. 'A rough and dangerous task'   13

 2. 'We were nearly stone mad … half crazy'   24

 3. 'Take up the cudgel … to remedy this
unfortunate village'   37

 4. 'Fairyland'   52

 5. 'Our state gets worse'   64

 6. 'The Hut'   72

 7. 'We rode on … carrying our revolvers in
our hands'   81

 8. 'He would not turn off his road for any Shinner'   98

 9. 'Blood was slowly trickling from his left ear'   112

10. 'Guilty of wilful murder'   127

11. 'This ambush ought not to have occurred'   140

12. 'What Dev did in Boland's Mills, Jack Flynn
did at Ballymacandy'   155

13. 'Honesty is the best of policy'   166

    Postscript – 'They are the fellows that put
    us here'   182

Appendix I: List of participants in the Ballymacandy
    Ambush, 1 June 1921   188

Appendix II: Members of Milltown District Council
    of Cumann na mBan, July 1921   194

Acknowledgements   196

Endnotes   199

Index   219

FOREWORD

In this welcome addition to the many books produced on the revolutionary period since this Decade of Centenaries began in 2012, Owen O'Shea takes a close look at one of many ambushes that occurred in Kerry during the War of Independence, 1919–21. Local studies, which uncover forgotten or marginalised details of contexts, personalities and events of this period, have become an important part of the processes of memory. Many studies have overlooked the local in favour of sweeping national narratives. While many incidents like the Ballymacandy Ambush lay half-remembered in local memories and oral history, the availability of digitised military pension applications and Bureau of Military History witness statements from the Irish Military Archives, as well as access to multiple other sources, allows researchers to dig deep, find the voices and reconstruct the immediate as well as the broad contexts for events.

O'Shea uses the eyewitness accounts of two young Milltown schoolboys, who, curious about the sounds of gunfire heard from the classroom on a blistering hot day in June 1921, ran towards those sounds rather than away from them, so setting the stage for this local history. The sight they came upon, dead bodies strewn on the road and a woman nearby, keening, was a scene never to be forgotten by either. However, in many ways the ambush at Ballymacandy was forgotten, at least in the mainstream and national narratives of trauma, war and violence. Now with greater access to archives, especially through the pension applications of members of the IRA and the women's association, Cumann na mBan, and with a deep knowledge of and connection to the area, O'Shea provides us with a masterful, detailed reconstruction of the context and detail of what happened that fateful day.

Five members of the Crown Forces were killed at Ballymacandy on 1 June 1921 by members of the 6th Battalion of the Kerry No.2 Brigade and the Active Service Unit (ASU) of the No.1 Brigade. O'Shea frames what happened here in the context of ongoing events in Kerry from the outbreak of violence post-1916, beginning with the first raid on an RIC barracks by Kerry Volunteers at Gortatlea on 13 April 1918. Irish Volunteer companies had been in place in Kerry from 1914, as had branches of Cumann na mBan. The Easter Rising had its own particular impact on Kerry, with the first deaths of 1916 happening at Ballykissane pier when Irish Volunteers, Con Keating, Daniel Sheehan and Charlie Monahan, drowned while on active service. Most famously, the German ship the *Aud* failed to deliver its cargo of arms – destined for use in the uprising – to the Kerry Volunteers and senior revolutionary leader Roger Casement, who was arrested near Banna on 21 April 1916.

O'Shea unpacks the complicated stories of Kerry, especially mid-Kerry, in the War of Independence. The boycott of the RIC, the arrival of the Black and Tans, the increasing numbers of young men and women joining the IRA and Cumann na mBan respectively, created a tense and volatile situation. By late 1920 parts of Kerry were only under a semblance of control by the

Crown Forces, and ambushes of the RIC at Hillville in October 1920, in which two constables were killed, and soon after at Kilderry, led to vicious Crown Force reprisals in Milltown and Killorglin. By the time of the ambush at Ballymacandy the pressure on the RIC was immense, and the guerrilla warfare conducted by Flying Columns with the assistance of Cumann na mBan was taking its toll.

In setting the scene for the Ballymacandy Ambush, O'Shea brings to life the men and women who were involved, on both sides. What stands out in this study are the parallel lives of RIC Sergeant James Collery and IRA leader Dan Mulvihill. By 1921 Collery was stationed in Killorgin RIC Barracks with a mixed force of RIC and Black and Tans, and Mulvihill was a senior member of the 6th Battalion of the Kerry No. 2 Brigade, IRA. The trajectories of their lives would bring the two men to a dramatic and violent encounter at Ballymacandy.

O'Shea evokes the complex political and societal relationships of people in the local communities in mid-Kerry in 1920–21. From active members of the IRA and Cumann na mBan, to local constables of the RIC, and members of the hated Black and Tans, to civilians – Protestant and Catholic, landowners and tenants, town-dwellers and rural inhabitants, all were caught up in and impacted by the conflict. He details the conflicted and uneasy position of the local Protestant landowners, the involvement of so many young men and women in militant republicanism, and the impossibility of policing communities during a guerrilla war when the civilian population was increasingly resistant to British rule and law. He also details the terror visited on communities by those forces of the Crown in official and unofficial reprisal attacks as well as the self-policing by republicans of their 'own' people – often violently, including the violence meted out to young women for 'company keeping' with members of the RIC or military.

What O' Shea has expertly produced here – using all available sources, from archive material and contemporary newspaper reports to eyewitness accounts – is a deep analysis of the social, political and revolutionary histories of his own community, centred round the impact of a single War of Independence ambush. Micro-histories such as these are vital to building up the layers of a broader narrative of the revolutionary period. Without understanding what motivated Dan Mulvihill and his sisters (who joined Cumann na mBan) and the other men and women of Kerry's revolutionary generation to take up the fight for Irish freedom, or why that fight led to Sergeant James Collery's violent death on a road in mid-Kerry in the summer of 1921, we cannot fully understand and acknowledge the histories, impacts and legacies of our revolutionary times. This is a fascinating and necessary story.

Dr Mary McAuliffe,
Assistant Professor in Gender Studies,
University College Dublin

PREFACE

As a student of politics, I often came across the famous Tip O'Neill quote that all politics is local. As a student of history, I often thought the same adage could be applied to that subject: all history is local too. The War of Independence of a century ago is, in many ways, a combination or varied tapestry of local histories, the sum of many parts. The ambushes, the burnings, the assaults, the shootings, the executions, the reprisals, the informing, the paranoia and the subterfuge, which played out in all their horror at a local level, combined to create and inform the wider national narrative of the Irish revolution.

As a child, I grew up listening to sporadic mentions of the ambush of the Black and Tans just a quarter of a mile from where I was born. The site of the ambush – and the subject of this book – is just a few fields away from where I grew up. Ballymacandy, however, meant little else to me as a child other than a place where my grand-aunt Nora and her husband Denis Murphy lived and which we often visited. As the centenary of the ambush approached, however, Ballymacandy took on a whole new meaning for me and I was determined to find out more about what happened there a century ago.

In approaching the subject, I was astonished that the deaths of five men on the road between Milltown and Castlemaine on 1 June 1921, just weeks before the War of Independence came to an end, was barely mentioned in histories of the period. It was often a mere footnote to accounts of the revolution in Kerry, despite the number of deaths and the scale of the involvement of IRA, Cumann na mBan and Fianna Éireann members from across mid-Kerry. Maybe the five men who died were considered just another of the statistics amid the thousand-plus people who died in Ireland as a result of the conflict in the first six months of 1921. And maybe those who led the attack were considered just another insignificant group of the many thousands of rebels who took up arms against the Crown Forces in these tumultuous years.

Further investigation showed that some of the information in the public domain was inconsistent and incorrect. I quickly discovered that, despite repeated references to the deaths of five Black and Tans, not all of those who died were 'Tans' at all. James Collery, the father of nine children who lived in my home village of Milltown, was as Irish as the men who killed him: but nowhere was there any mention of who he was, where he came from and how and why he died. Moreover, Collery's assailants and those who fired upon the police patrol were mentioned in anecdotes and local folk memory but their stories had never been adequately documented before.

In my approach to researching the ambush, I made a conscientious effort to tell both sides of the story, to present the accounts of the protagonists and eyewitnesses, allowing readers to consider what happened and develop their own interpretations and understandings of events one hundred years on. I quickly realised, however, that the history of the War of Independence is not just about 'both sides'. This tumultuous and traumatic period in the history of our country and the community I grew up in has many 'sides' – the perspective of the IRA gunmen, the RIC constables, the Black and Tans, the ordinary civilians in the villages of Milltown and Castlemaine, the women of Cumann na mBan who carried and hid guns, the priest who prayed into the ears of the dying, the woman widowed by the ambush, the IRA's informer within the police, the schoolboys who watched as bloodied remains were loaded onto carts and the doctor accused of neglecting a dying man.

Throughout my research, I was struck by the generosity and enthusiasm of the descendants of the people who feature on these pages. Remarkably, many descendants admitted that they did not know the extent of the involvement of their loved ones in these events and are only now learning about what their ancestors did at this momentous time in our history. There was, however, a combination of gratitude and pride that someone was willing to tell their story. Boxes of medals were produced from cupboards, pictures taken down from mantelpieces, handwritten letters retrieved from shoeboxes. But there was also a constant and enduring refrain: 'They didn't really talk about what happened.'

Thankfully, long after many of those who participated in these events passed from this world, their accounts in the Bureau of Military History and the Military Archives are being published and made available to students, historians and the relatives of those involved. So too, through police records in the British Archives, do we get an insight into the lives and activities of the members of the Royal Irish Constabulary, the Auxiliaries and the Black and Tans. Reading and deciphering these accounts and forensically weaving together the complexities of those stories has been a revelation and a thrill.

The accounts elucidated here have, I hope, greatly helped to address the 'knowledge deficit' in relation to the War of Independence, which historian Charles Townshend wrote about twenty years ago. He added, however, that even at this remove 'objectivity may still be more difficult to achieve'.[1] Perhaps objectivity is impossible; even if, in recent years, the War of Independence has 'loosened its grip on the Irish psyche'.[2] Diarmaid Ferriter has noted that we now know more about this turbulent period in our history, 'but that does not mean we can easily achieve an untangling of its knotted legacy or rise above the emotion it still generates'.[3]

Trying forever to reach some utopian objectivity should not, however, be a barrier to discussing, probing, learning, writing about and documenting our important and precious collective history. A century on, I hope that this account of what happened on the roads and in the fields near my homeplace, and this telling of an important and traumatic moment in the history of my community, that of County Kerry and of the country, gives a voice to the men and women who were involved and who witnessed these turbulent events and lived through such historic and pivotal times. I hope that it offers a story that deserves and requires to be told in all its tangled, complicated and emotive manifestations.

PROLOGUE – *SALVE REGINA*

Brother Paulinus stepped onto the rostrum and hushed the classroom. The last half hour of the schoolday for the senior boys at the Monastery School in Milltown was usually set aside for singing. It was Wednesday, 1 June 1921 and the boys on the second floor of the school adjacent to the Church of the Sacred Heart had their minds on their usual carefree post-school antics as the clock ticked towards four. It was 'another listless, enervating day of scorching heat' typical of many during what was a long, warm summer of 1921.[1] Brother Paulinus was a member of the large community of Presentation Brothers who were resident in Milltown at the time. In 1841 the Presentation Sisters – who had established a presence in Milltown just a few years earlier – and the local parish priest, Fr Batt O'Connor, had invited the Brothers, whose order was founded by Edmund Ignatius Rice, to establish a school to educate the boys of the parish.[2] Like so many religious orders in Ireland at the time, the Presentation Brothers filled a void in the delivery of education and provided a wide range of social services that were not otherwise available. By the early 1860s the Brothers' school in Milltown has developed a strong educational reputation and had been dubbed 'The Little Academy'.[3] By 1921, the school had 130 boys on its roll.

A native Irish speaker from the Coolea area of west Cork and a staunch supporter of the Irish cultural movement which prevailed at the time, Brother Paulinus was instrumental in organising Irish plays, recitations and other sociocultural events in the 1920s with the support of local school principals like James Lambe of Callinafercy National School and Denis Healy of Rockfield National School.[4] In his approach to the teaching of singing, and as a steadfast nationalist, Brother Paulinus 'had long put aside the stereotyped melodies that were at the period part and parcel of the school curriculum under the English Educational system' and favoured ballads with a more republican bent.[5] His favourite anthems included 'O'Donnell Abú', 'The Green Flag' and 'The Men of the West'. With the War of Independence or the so-called 'Tan War' raging in mid-Kerry and around Ireland, and as the Irish Republican Army took their guerrilla warfare campaign against the Crown Forces towards its climax, the Presentation monk was inclined to sing such songs with an added gusto. His pupils, according to one of them, 'always gave full vent to their vocal cords in the stirring strains of those grand martial airs'.[6] 'And again, boys,' he implored:

I give you the gallant old West, boys,
Where rallied our bravest and best
When Ireland lay broken and bleeding;
Hurrah for the men of the West!

As the singing concluded, Brother Paulinus led the class in the daily ritual of praying *The Litany of the Blessed Virgin*, and finally, to complete the songs and psalms, the best of Latin intonations were invoked for the *Salve Regina*:

Salve, Regina, Mater misericordiae,
vita, dulcedo, et spes nostra, salve.
Ad te clamamus exsules filii Hevae,
Ad te suspiramus, gementes et flentes
in hac lacrimarum valle …

A few lines into the prayer, the first gunshots resounded from about a mile away. Despite the ongoing war and occasional outbreaks of violence in the locality, the sound of shooting was relatively rare in the Milltown area, which had been largely spared the worst excesses of the recent combat. Schoolboy Denis Sugrue later recounted:

> Through the open windows … came the sounds of rifle fire from the direction of the Castlemaine road. There was a whisper among the lads that it must be an ambush, for some of them had seen the cycling patrol of police going towards Tralee that morning, on their way to school. There was a rush for the door, but Brother Paulinus kept us in our places until the firing had died away. He then ordered us to go home as quickly as we could.[7]

When the gunfire had ended, many of the boys ran to their homes but curiosity got the better of two of the schoolboys, Denis Sugrue and his friend Thomas 'Totty' O'Sullivan. Fear of what might await them or the warnings of Brother Paulinus were not going to deter the pair from a chance to witness the fighting, which they had been hearing about for months from their elders and neighbours in the hushed conversations of homes and shops around the village. They ran to the Castlemaine

Road. They rounded the bend at Rathpook and came to the straight section of road at Ballymacandy about a mile from the village to discover a shocking sight: 'For us young lads it was an eerie atmosphere with the odour of gunpowder polluting the air. There were dead men lying on the road, and the only sign of life was the long figure of a woman crooning over the strewn bodies.'[8] It was a scene 'never to be forgotten'.[9]

Ballymacandy Ambush

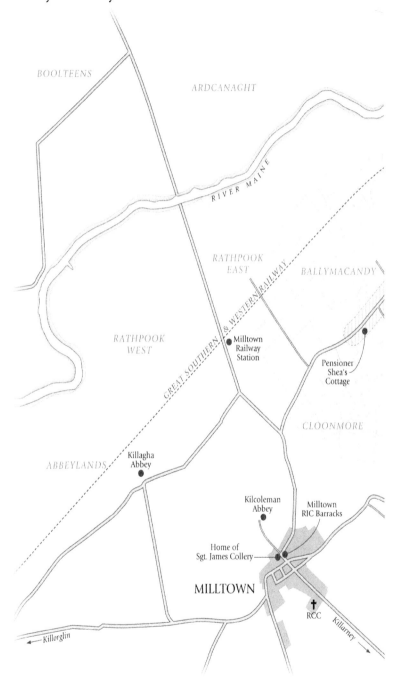

BOOLTEENS

ARDCANAGHT

RIVER MAINE

RATHPOOK
EAST

BALLYMACANDY

GREAT SOUTHERN & WESTERN RAILWAY

RATHPOOK
WEST

● Milltown
Railway
Station

Pensioner
Shea's
Cottage

CLOONMORE

ABBEYLANDS

Killagha
Abbey
●

Kilcoleman
Abbey
●

Milltown
RIC Barracks

Home of
Sgt. James Collery →

MILLTOWN

RCC

Killarney →

← Killorglin

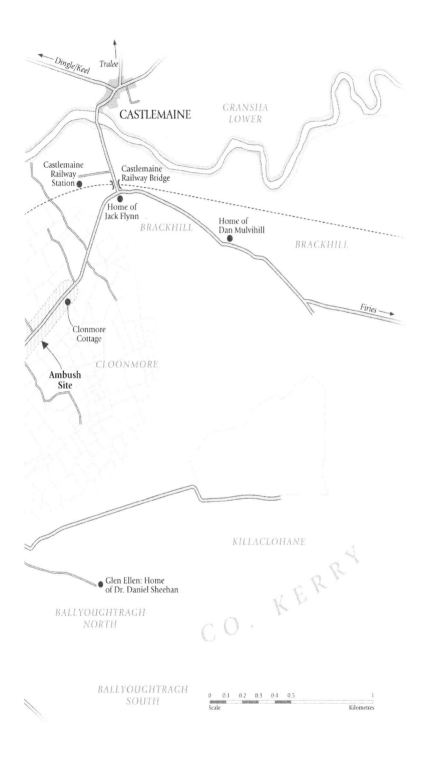

1

'A ROUGH AND DANGEROUS TASK'

It is often claimed that the War of Independence began in Kerry.[1] That is perhaps apposite given that the first tragic episode of the Easter Rising of 1916 had been played out in the county a few short years before. Indeed, it was not a great distance from Ballymacandy – the stage for the drama which plays out in this book – that three men drowned in what is considered the first set of casualties of the ill-fated rebellion. When the car in which they were travelling plunged into Castlemaine harbour, having been accidentally driven off the end of Ballykissane pier near Killorglin, the freezing water claimed the lives of Irish Volunteer members Daniel Sheehan, Charles Monahan and Con Keating early on Good Friday morning in 1916. Kerry would make its own significant and often overlooked contribution to the seismic events of the remainder of that momentous Easter weekend.[2] It was two years later, almost to the day, that the gunshots – those which are arguably the first of the War of Independence, or the Anglo-Irish War – were fired in a remote townland in Kerry, heralding a new period in the military conflict with the representatives of British rule in Ireland. The assault by the Ballymacelligott Company of the Irish Volunteers on the barracks of the Royal Irish Constabulary at Gortatlea in the parish of Ballymacelligott in April 1918 marked, if not the beginning of, then certainly a significant gear shift in the republican war with His Majesty's Constabulary in County Kerry. Gortatlea was, as Martin Moore has written, a 'daring attack, as nothing like it had been attempted since the [Easter] Rising'.[3]

'The next few years,' after 1918, wrote Kerry IRA Volunteer, Jeremiah Murphy, 'were amongst the most momentous in Irish history and produced examples of courage, betrayal, murder, pillage, ambush and tyranny not experienced since the rebellion of 1798.'[4] The rout of Irish Parliamentary Party MPs in the face of a Sinn Féin surge at the December 1918 general election – against the background of the Conscription Crisis – dramatically transformed the political landscape. As the new independent parliament, Dáil Éireann, met for the first time on 21 January 1919, what were more widely credited as the first shots of the War of Independence were being fired in Soloheadbeg in County Tipperary. It would be the following year before the conflict really escalated in Kerry, however.

While it is neither the intention nor the ambition of this book to provide a detailed account of the War of Independence in Kerry and outline every single event in the years before the ambush at Ballymacandy, it will examine some of the key incidents in the mid-Kerry area in which the members of the IRA honed their skills and tactics in confronting the enemy. It will also consider who that enemy was, and how policing had changed so inexorably in Ireland by 1921, so that we might better understand how both sides in the conflict came to engage so violently with each other on the road between Milltown and Castlemaine on 1 June 1921.

For almost a century before the outbreak of the War of Independence in 1919, the upholding of law and order in Ireland had been entrusted to the Irish Constabulary, which was established in 1822. The 'Royal' prefix was added in 1867 in recognition by Queen Victoria of the force's suppression of the Fenian Rising. In the later part of the nineteenth century, public perception of the police force varied 'according to the level of unrest in Ireland at the time'.[5] While it was associated with the brutality of evictions of the Famine and the Land War, by the turn of the century, the RIC was 'an indigenous civil police force, which habitually policed without arms and carried out routine policing functions'.[6] The force was preoccupied for the most part with ordinary and mundane policing tasks: it had become 'a civil police force which reflected the socio-economic structure of Irish society in its composition and in its operations, the needs of small, relatively law-abiding, rural communities'.[7] Former Kerry Garda Chief Superintendent Donal O'Sullivan notes that the RIC was a force which had the broad acceptance and support of the population and largely had the interests of the communities it served at heart.[8] In her history of the IRA in Kerry, Sinéad Joy attributes the reasonably good relationship between the police and the policed to the provincial nature of Kerry society, the fact that many RIC members came from 'good farming stock' as well as the attraction of the police as a career option where emigration was often the only other choice.[9] A career in the RIC proved appealing to many young

Irish men. At the beginning of 1920, there were almost 10,000 members in 1,300 detachments across the country. The role offered a position of status in the community; it was a well-paid job with promotional opportunities; boots and the distinctive bottle-green uniform were supplied free of charge; and married men received a lodging allowance.[10] RIC historian Jim Herlihy explains the place the force occupied in the careers landscape for a young Irishman in the nineteenth and early twentieth centuries: 'The rural population produced large families and it was often usual for one son to remain on the farm, a few to emigrate to America, one perhaps to enter the priesthood and one or more sons to join the Constabulary as it was considered to be "a job for life".'[11]

Among those attracted to a career in the Royal Irish Constabulary was James Collery.[12] Born James Christopher Collery on 27 November 1875 in the townland of Killavil, Ballymote, County Sligo, just a few miles from the Mayo border, he was the youngest of six children born to farmer Patrick Collery and his wife Anne (née O'Gara).[13] In many ways, Collery was typical of the type of young man who joined the RIC: police historian Elizabeth Malcolm observes that recruits to the constabulary were usually found among the sons, especially the younger sons, of small farming families in the south, west and midlands and that they were usually unmarried and Catholic.[14] James Collery satisfied all of these criteria: he was a farmer's son, was the youngest son of a family of six, was a Roman Catholic, and, at the time he joined the RIC in 1899, was not married. His older brother Michael also joined the police. James Collery entered the constabulary at the lowest rank at the time, that of constable, and he was a policeman of twenty years' experience when the War of Independence began. Collery was first posted to County Clare in February 1899 before being moved to Kerry on 1 December 1907.[15] Just a few months before his arrival in Kerry he had married Catherine Collins, a native of Doonaha in County Clare. A photographic portrait of their marriage is dated 10 September 1907.

Collery's assignment to various police barracks in Kerry was in keeping with a general policy of appointing RIC members to counties other than their own. He was stationed in Killarney and Glencar before moving to Milltown in 1908. The 1911 Census of Population lists Collery as residing at Main Street, Milltown, along with his then thirty-year-old wife, Catherine, and two children: Anne, aged two, and a baby, also called Catherine.[16] He is also listed on the 1911 Census return for the RIC Barracks at Main Street, Milltown, under the initials 'J.C.' in line with the practice whereby only the initials of police officers were provided on the census forms.[17] James and Catherine Collery would go on to have seven more children, many of whom were educated by the Presentation Brothers and Sisters in the village. A picture of the Presentation Convent School pupils from 1912 includes the smiling face of Anne Collery, surrounded by her classmates and under the watchful eye of Sisters Xavier Purcell and Theresa Shanahan.[18] James Collery must have impressed his superiors because on 1 April 1919 he was promoted to the rank of sergeant at Milltown RIC Barracks.

By this point in his career Collery would have been in receipt of a salary of £260 per annum along with a weekly supplement of 13s. and 6d., which was paid to married officers.[19] While many of his colleagues resided in the barracks, married men did not, and James and Catherine reared their family in a large rented home at the Square in Milltown near the gated entrance to the demesne of the local former landlords, the Godfreys of Kilcoleman Abbey.[20] It appears the Collerys were generally well liked. Local historian Pat McKenna recalls: 'My aunt Lena told me that the Collerys were a lovely family and that they were very popular locally. In fact, her friend Maggie [O'Shea] acted as a godmother to some of the children at their baptisms.'[21]

All changed, changed utterly for James Collery and his colleagues with the outbreak of the War of Independence at the beginning of 1919 and particularly, a realisation by the British government that its Irish constabulary was unable – and in many cases unwilling – to provide meaningful resistance to a new rebel uprising against the Crown. As Volunteer, and later IRA violence increased, it became quickly apparent that the RIC was equipped with neither the manpower nor the skills to cope with a guerrilla campaign of ambushes, shootings and raids. The RIC was simply 'not up to the job' and were 'unprepared for what lay ahead'.[22] Any organisation associated with British rule in Ireland inevitably and invariably became identified with efforts to suppress and subvert the struggle for independence, especially when the War of Independence began. In 1919 fifteen RIC members were killed in combat, a figure which rose dramatically to 179 in 1920.[23] Many officers who were eligible for a pension began to leave the force in 1920 and in increasing numbers. Recruitment slowed as young men who were eligible to join looked for other, safer careers at a time when RIC members were being targeted and their families often threatened or intimidated by the IRA.[24] This rise in police casualties, an increasing demoralisation in the force, the closure of many rural police stations (an easy target for the IRA) and a flood of retirements prompted an appeal to London by army leader Field Marshal Henry Wilson for more manpower and resources. Kerry was identified in April 1919, along with several other counties, as requiring additional boots on the ground due to a general state of disturbance.[25] The result was the creation of a new Division of the Royal Irish Constabulary as well as the introduction of the infamous 'Black and Tans'.

'Kerry got an awful hammering from the Tans and Auxiliaries,' is how Tralee IRA man Billy Mullins described the impact of two of the most dreaded and notorious military forces ever deployed anywhere in the world.[26] 'Tan' was the nickname given to the thousands of ex-servicemen who were recruited by the British government in 1920 and 1921 in an attempt to shore up the military presence in Ireland. Their uniforms were a dark green (which appeared almost black) and khaki-brown or tan colour, leading to the genesis of the Black and Tan epithet, and came about partly because it was impossible to provide sufficient quantities of the regular dark-green RIC uniform.[27] With pay of ten shillings a day, the new force was created as a 'special emergency gendarmerie, which was heavily armed, motorised, and organised in military-style companies'.[28] Contrary perhaps to some perceptions, the Black and Tans were not exclusively English, with significant numbers being recruited in Ireland.[29] There was a surge in recruits in the autumn of 1920 as a deep post-war recession took hold in Britain. Most Black and Tans had served in the army during the First World War and were in their early twenties. RIC officers tended to live in their barracks; the Tans lived and worked with them and, by the spring of 1921, the average garrison was home to members of both police bodies.

The Black and Tans became a law unto themselves. They had no training in routine police work, found it difficult to conform to the discipline inherent in the RIC and did not always willingly accept instruction from senior RIC officers. As Fergal Keane records in his book on events in north Kerry in this period, the Black and Tans were renowned by some as 'the sweepings of British jails: to a man they were murderers, cut throats, and rapists in the long inglorious line of Elizabeth I's pillagers, Cromwell's butchers and the gibbet-wearing redcoats'.[30] The Sinn Féin TD for East Kerry Piaras Béaslaí called the Black and Tans 'the dregs of the population of English cities'.[31] In recent times however, there have been more rounded assessments of the force. Black-and-Tans historian D.M. Leeson suggests, for example, that members were not the jailbirds and down-and-outs of Irish republican folklore. Most of them, he says, were quite ordinary men.[32] William Sheehan adds that they were not the dregs of British prisons but ex-servicemen, many of whom had distinguished war records.[33] Condemnation and fear of the Black and Tans was not universal. There were some, albeit very few, reports of a 'great spirit of friendliness' between Black and Tans and civilians in Killorglin, while Bertie Scully of the Glencar IRA recalled that they were 'not bad to prisoners' locally.[34]

Alongside the Black and Tans was the Auxiliary Division of the RIC (ADRIC), better known as the Auxiliaries and usually 'Auxies' for short. In theory, they were an ancillary division of the constabulary, but in reality, they operated as 'an independent strike force' with the clear objective of taking the war to the IRA.[35] ADRIC was formed in mid-1920 and was a force of 8,000 members, the vast majority of whom were soldiers. Auxiliaries tended to wear a dark-blue uniform with a Glengarry cap and a crowned harp as a badge. They also wore a bandolier and were usually equipped with a revolver, a rifle and up to fifty rounds of ammunition.[36] One in ten Auxiliaries was Irish-born.[37] The Auxiliaries also operated a regime largely unfettered by the norms of policing or the rules of warfare. Increasingly infuriated by the withdrawal of the IRA from urban areas and into the wilderness of rural Ireland where they were difficult to apprehend, the target for the Auxiliaries' anger and frustration became civilians and their property, particularly if they were related to or connected to men on the run. Not long after their arrival in Kerry, an incident in east Kerry exemplified the reign of terror with which the Auxies came to be associated:

One day a small party of Auxiliaries in a lorry stopped at the neighbouring village of Gneevegullia. They made a quick search of a few homes for no apparent reason, but this was not unusual. They noticed a picture of the [Irish] volunteers of 1914 in one house, and the man of the house among them. He was questioned about his IRA connections and though he was not implicated since 1914, he was arrested. His house was burned to the ground and he was taken away. When the lorry reached Tralee his legs were tied to the tailgate and his head dragged along the road. 'He had been shot while trying to escape' or so his captors claimed.[38]

The first 500 Auxiliaries arrived in Dublin at the end of July 1920 and by the end of October 1920 an ADRIC company of 100 men had been formed in Kerry.[39] They were based at Moyderwell Technical School in Tralee under the command of the notorious Lt John Alistair Mackinnon. Mackinnon would become synonymous with the worst brutalities of the war in the county and, from the moment he arrived in Kerry, he was a marked man.

The effect on the RIC of the introduction of the Black and Tans and the Auxiliaries was immense, and for many of its members, incredibly dangerous. As the war intensified, the RIC became part of what Fergal Keane called the 'messy amalgam' of policing in Ireland: the uniform, whether worn by James Collery's RIC or members of the Black and Tans or Auxiliaries, became the symbol of the increasingly suppressive and violent regime being imposed from London.[40] In effect, the policeman – whether he be RIC, Auxiliary or Black and Tan – became one and the same thing in Ireland. In Clare, for example, where Tomás Mac Conmara has charted the revolutionary period, there was a consistent categorisation of all the police forces as Black and Tans or simply 'Tans'.[41] By the autumn of 1920 the *Killarney Echo and South Kerry Chronicle* claimed that the average RIC man had become an almost hermit-like outcast in his own community:

THE IRISH PARIAH

He has now no friends, and young women shun him. In his barrack he shelters himself behind steel shutters and sandbags; he has disappeared from hundreds of square miles of country; he carries his life in his hands, and when he is shot none except relatives mourn him, and in numerous instances undertakers have refused to supply the coffin with hearse for his burial. It is forbidden to speak to him, and to associate with him is a high crime and misdemeanour. He walks abroad with the expectation of instant death; he salutes no one, and no one salutes him.[42]

The demonisation of the longer-serving constabulary through the arrival of the Black and Tans and the Auxiliaries, and the inevitable association between them and their more aggressive and bloody-minded colleagues caused serious divisions within the ranks of policing in Ireland. This tension between the peace-keeping tradition of the ordinary RIC men and the new warmongering swagger of the Tans and the Auxies would have explosive consequences, including a dramatic confrontation at the RIC barracks in Milltown in the summer of 1920, setting RIC Constable James Collery on a bloody collision course with his neighbours in the IRA.

2

'WE WERE NEARLY STONE MAD ... HALF CRAZY'

Daniel Mulvihill – one of the most senior and important members of the Irish Republican Army in Kerry in the early 1920s – credits his mother, Nora, with first nurturing his interest in Irish nationalism.[1] Like many young men who were inspired and motivated to take up arms against the British Empire at the beginning of the twentieth century, it was this introduction in the family home to the story of injustice, oppression and a history of rebellions in their native land that encouraged Mulvihill to join the armed struggle to achieve an independent Irish republic.

Mulvihill claimed that his mother was 'one of the greatest Irishwomen I ever knew. She never spared anything during the Tan time and Civil War. She knew more about Irish history than anyone I have ever met since.'[2] Mrs Mulvihill taught her children to be proud of their Irish heritage and to defend it: so successful was she in that endeavour that all six of them (four boys and two girls) became involved in the Irish Volunteers or Cumann na mBan. The family home would become a busy – and dangerous – hub of activity for republicans between 1919 and 1921 and during the Civil War thereafter, and was the launching pad for many attacks on the Crown Forces.

Daniel (Dan) Mulvihill was born in 1897, one of six children born to Cornelius and Nora, and grew up on a 120-acre farm at Brackhill on the outskirts of the village of Castlemaine. Mulvihill claimed to be descended from the Coleens and 'Black Mulvihills' of north Kerry who, in the nineteenth century, had been involved in the widespread practice of faction fighting and who took part in the so-called 'Battle of Ballyeagh' of 1834 in which dozens of participants were brutally killed.[3]

Brackhill, bordering the banks of the River Maine, was part of the parish of Milltown. The family farm was a relatively large holding for rural Kerry at the time and the 1911 Census, for example, records the presence of a 21-year-old servant, Laurence Shea, at the family home.[4] However, Shea's presence may have had more to do with the premature death of Dan's father, Cornelius. Mulvihill left home in the summer of 1915 to learn wireless radio and Morse code at a school run by his cousin in Kilrush, County Clare.[5] He was admitted to the Marconi School of Wireless at Chelmsford in London in April 1916, in the same week as the Irish Republican Brotherhood (IRB) and the Irish Volunteers were taking up their position in the General Post Office in Dublin to rebel against British occupation in Ireland in what became known as the Easter Rising. There is no evidence in his own papers and testimonies, however, that Mulvihill was becoming more politicised at this stage or involved in the myriad Irish cultural and political organisations in London, which provided such a fertile breeding ground for many of the leaders of the campaign for Irish independence.[6]

On a brief return to Ireland at the end of 1916, Mulvihill joined a Sinn Féin club established during a meeting at the old dispensary in Milltown.[7] In his two years in London, however, the young Mulvihill seemed more interested in city life, lying in the sun reading science fiction in Hyde Park and under Marble Arch and attending the movie theatres and West End shows while earning a living as a radio operator at Marconi House, headquarters of the Marconi companies at The Strand. He became friendly with an amateur pilot with whom he flew in a biplane several times and at this point even contemplated a career in the air corps. Mulvihill's contemplation of a career in the Royal Air Force may have been no more than youthful flirtation with the anticipated exhilaration of a job as a fighter pilot but it also belies any romantic notion that those who fought the Black and Tans in 1920–21 followed a universal personal and career trajectory, participation in and politicisation through various political and cultural organisations, all usually leading to the ultimate taking-up of arms. Even as the Irish Volunteers began to take the fight to the Crown Forces in 1918–19 in Kerry and elsewhere, and as the Conscription Crisis raged at home, Dan Mulvihill was travelling the world with little apparent ambition to be involved in the fate of his fellow countrymen at home. In August 1918 he took up a post as a radio operator on a steamship, travelling to the Gulf of Mexico and docking at exotic locations like Galveston, Havana and Buenos Aires: he 'liked the wandering from port to port'.[8] By the end of 1918, however, he was forced to return to Brackhill. His older brother Patrick was ill with tuberculosis, which he had contracted during the Great Flu pandemic. Realising his duty to take over the running of the family farm, Dan Mulvihill gave up his career as a radio operator and, on the advice of his dying brother, went to study agriculture in Clonakilty in County Cork. It was there that he first became interested and ultimately involved in the republicanism that would lead him into a lethal conflict with the Crown Forces on the road near his home on 1 June 1921.

Companies of Irish Volunteers had been established very rapidly across Kerry following the foundation of the organisation on 25 November 1913 at the Rotunda in Dublin, as the campaign for Home Rule in Ireland intensified. In mid-Kerry companies were formed in Milltown in March 1914, Killorglin in May, Keel in June and Glenbeigh in July.[9] Callinafercy, a large townland between Killorglin and Milltown, established its own company in the spring of 1917. A company was also formed in Kiltallagh, which encompassed much of the greater Castlemaine area. In the years after the Easter Rising the Volunteers reorganised and transformed into the Irish Republican Army which, during the War of Independence, would dislodge Crown governance across most of Ireland and bring military control of the country to a standstill by 1920–21.[10] The local rural company of the Volunteers and subsequently the IRA was structured around the parish boundaries of dioceses of the Catholic Church. These local companies came together to form battalions, largely based on districts that made up Dáil constituencies, and a group of battalions were combined to form a brigade, which usually encompassed a large part of a county. Finally, those battalions were overseen by a division of the IRA – in the case of the Kerry battalions, the 1st Southern Division.

By 1920-21 County Kerry was divided into three brigade areas: Kerry No.1 Brigade encompassing north and west Kerry including Tralee; Kerry No.2 Brigade covering east Kerry, Killarney, much of mid-Kerry and the Kenmare area; and Kerry No.3 Brigade, which was based in the southern half of the Iveragh Peninsula and included the Cahersiveen area. Companies in the mid-Kerry area and those involved in the events at the centre of this book were scattered across a number of different battalion areas. The 2nd Battalion of Kerry No.2 Brigade, for example, included companies in Kiltallagh, Keel, Firies, Currans, Ashill and Ballymacelligott; the 4th Battalion included companies in Listry, Ballyhar, Beaufort and the Black Valley; and the 6th Battalion comprised the IRA companies from Milltown, Killorglin, Callinafercy, Dungeel, Glenbeigh, Kilgobnet and Caragh Lake.[11] From November 1920 the Officer Commanding (O/C) the 6th Battalion was Thomas (Tom) O'Connor of Milltown. Born in the same year as Dan Mulvihill at Knockreigh, Milltown, O'Connor had joined the Volunteers in 1916 and was imprisoned in 1918 at the time of the so-called German Plot. He recalled that so appalling and traumatic were the conditions in jail that 'one or two of the lads were removed to the Mental Hospital'.[12] O'Connor would lead the men of the mid-Kerry area through the turmoil and trauma of the Anglo-Irish War, ably assisted by his adjutant, Dan Mulvihill. At the other end of the Milltown parish, the Listry Company was part of the 4th Battalion of the Kerry No.2 Brigade, which gravitated towards east Kerry, Killarney and Ballymacelligott. The most prominent figure in the movement in the Listry area was Dan Allman of Rockfield, who would become a nationally well-known republican leader following his death at the Headford Junction Ambush on 21 March 1921. His brother Pat was also a member of the Listry Company, which despite being part of the No.2 Brigade was often involved closely with O'Connor, Mulvihill and the Milltown IRA in their engagements with the enemy. At the beginning of 1921 the Listry Company included some 125 members under Pat Allman's command.[13] Volunteer Daniel Healy, who was married to the Allmans' sister, noted that 'Daniel Allman was the moving spirit in the Volunteers in our area, and it was he who organised the Rockfield–Listry area … [he] lost no opportunity in trying to get a crack at the Tans.'[14]

At the end of 1919 Dan Mulvihill 'fell in' with the Milltown company of the IRA. His brother Patrick, by then qualified as a doctor, died of TB on 1 December 1919 and Dan was at home with his mother and sisters for several weeks. He had already joined the Volunteers while at agricultural college in southwest Cork, where he had been immersed in Gaelic games. But it was the local IRA company in Clonakilty, and one of its members in particular, which became a key influence. Jim Hurley would later play inter-county football and hurling with Cork but during the revolutionary period he became one of the most prominent IRA figures in west Cork. Hurley was the leader of a Flying Column with the 3rd Cork Brigade. He was a member of the ambush party during the Civil War that launched the attack at Beál na mBláth on 22 August 1922 in which Michael Collins was killed.[15] Hurley and Mulvihill were also involved in scuffles with British soldiers in Clonakilty in May 1920. By July that year Mulvihill was home. 'The Black and Tans had just arrived. There was a lull, calm before the storm, everyone waiting.'[16] From here on in, he was 'out [the] whole time'.

For a small, sparsely populated rural townland in mid-Kerry, Brackhill produced a disproportionately large number of IRA Volunteers. These included brothers James (Jimmy), John and Daniel Cronin, as well as a neighbour, Denis Dowd.[17] Chief among the Brackhill contingent was John 'Jack' Flynn, who lived a few fields away from the Mulvihill homestead in a large farmhouse. The property overlooked Castlemaine railway station and the strategically important junction of the road which ran through Castlemaine village and the main Milltown to Firies road. Flynn, along with his brothers Edward and James, was immersed in the Volunteers and the IRA from a young age. Jack Flynn was an athlete, singer and musician of some renown, which earned him the nickname 'Fiddler Flynn': he would later enter politics, serving as a county councillor and Teachta Dála for Fianna Fáil.[18] Jack Flynn and Dan Mulvihill would operate hand in glove in the years that followed. Like the Flynns' home, the Mulvihill home also became a safe house – a refuge for IRA Volunteers on the run.[19] Hardly a night went by, Mulvihill noted, that there was not 'some stranger' staying at their home. The Mulvihill sisters joined Cumann na mBan where they 'did a lot of work in the line of dispatches' and took care of IRA members on the run.[20] 'We were,' explained Dan Mulvihill, 'nearly stone mad', 'half crazy' and always 'playing tricks on one another.'[21]

The men of Brackhill, like many of the IRA's recruits, certainly had no military experience or training so General

Headquarters (GHQ) assisted local brigades in training members on tactics such as the cutting and digging up of roads to disrupt transportation of police and British soldiers, scouting for the enemy, making gunpowder and bombs and the use of guns and ammunition. Those weapons and ammunition were greatly lacking in many companies: in the summer of 1921, for example, the fifty or so members of the Keel Company of the IRA had just ten weapons between them.[22] In the absence of the importation of arms, local units were largely left to their own devices to acquire weapons, which in itself prompted many of the raids on police barracks and the 'big houses' as well as ambushes of the Crown forces, which became increasingly frequent during 1920–21. But if they were lacking in guns, IRA members came to rely on other weapons including 'stealth, audaciousness, ingenuity, patience, diligence, dedication and discipline', all of which combined to make the IRA remarkably successful in taking on the might of the Crown forces in Ireland.[23]

In the summer and autumn of 1920, Dan Mulvihill and his comrades were getting a proper taste of combat: this occurred against a backdrop of increasing national IRA activity and led, in Kerry and neighbouring counties, to the declaration of martial law by the end of the year. One of Mulvihill's first actions was an attempt to burn the RIC barracks in Milltown on 10 August 1920.

The barracks had just recently been vacated by the RIC – who had moved to another building in the village – and the IRA wanted to make their mark. They set out, Mulvihill recalled, to try to make it 'uninhabitable' but 'we made a bad job of it as we had no explosives and burning [the barracks] meant burning other houses'.[24] A week later Mulvihill got his first experience of an ambush, a technique that increasingly became part of the IRA modus operandi as the War of Independence dragged on. On 16 August 1920, just a week after the Restoration of Order in Ireland Act was passed by Parliament in Westminster, IRA companies in mid-Kerry planned an ambush of Black and Tans – newly arrived in Ireland and in County Kerry – as they travelled on the main road between Killorglin and Killarney. A steep slip road that joined the main road near Beaufort Bridge was selected to place a horse cart which, at the right time, would be rolled down the hill into the path of the Black and Tans to block their journey. This sort of entrapment of police patrols by the placement of obstructions on a roadway was commonplace and, when successful, afforded the attackers the opportunity to fire on their targets. As they waited for their prey, Mulvihill noticed a party of civilians on horseback below the IRA vantage point who were travelling from the Killarney direction and across Beaufort bridge. Among the group was the American writer, journalist and adventurer Negley Farson and his wife, Enid Eveleen (née Stoker), a niece of Bram Stoker, the author of *Dracula*. The couple had been staying at Flesk Castle in Killarney and may well have been on the way to The Reeks in Beaufort, home of the McGillycuddy of the Reeks, whose mother, Agnes, was married to Enid's uncle, Dr George Stoker. A quarter of a century later Farson recounted the episode in his autobiography, *The Way Of A Transgressor*: 'We went up on horseback through the Gap of Dunloe – riding within three yards of a Sinn Féin ambush that an hour later bushwhacked some British officers.'[25] The officers were not 'bushwhacked' at all, however. As the Tans approached in their motorcar from

Killarney, the signal was given and the cart was released down the hill but it 'only went forward about two feet and stopped'.[26] The Tans drove onwards and escaped a grenade thrown in the direction of their car. The IRA men scattered in expectation of a police sweep of the district.

The role of the women's organisation Cumann na mBan in the revolutionary period has been largely overlooked and understated in much of the history of the time but is central to what happened at Ballymacandy and during similar incidents in mid-Kerry. The important contribution made by women, particularly during the War of Independence, has only recently received the focus it deserves, thanks in part to the many hundreds of military pension applications made by members of the organisation, some of which have been published in recent years. Formed in 1914, and with a clear aim to 'advance the cause of Irish liberty and to organise Irishwomen in the furtherance of this object', branches of the organisation were gradually established in Kerry including in Dingle and Tralee in 1915.[27] RIC estimates put the number of branches in Kerry at the outbreak of the War of Independence at eleven with a membership of 327 but one study has put membership in Kerry at around 2,000, accounting for some 12 per cent of the national total.[28] John P Heffernan, captain of the Callinafercy Company, known locally as 'Jack Captain', insisted that it 'would be impossible for the [Flying] Column to have lived in this area if it was not for the Cumann na mBan'.[29] In mid-Kerry, many hundreds of women joined Cumann na mBan. The Milltown District Council, formed in 1918, had almost forty members in the summer of 1921.[30] A handwritten list of names of the members was published in recent years by the Military Archives and lists May Allman of Rockfield, sister of IRA members Daniel and Patrick Allman, as O/C, Nellie Corcoran as 1st Lieutenant and Kathy Healy as 2nd Lieutenant (see Appendix 2).

Thanks to the availability now of the accounts of some of these women, we are able to develop a better insight into their activities, their responsibilities and their motives and to cast a light on the huge risks to their safety and their lives associated with their work at the time. The home of Margaret Slattery at Lyre Cottage near Milltown, for example, was a regular meeting place for IRA and Cumann na mBan members. Margaret joined the Milltown Council of the organisation about 1918 and became company captain soon after. Her father and brothers were active in the IRA and each served time in jail. Among Slattery's main duties were raising money, making haversacks, first aid, carrying dispatches and gathering intelligence.[31] Slattery explained that she had 'travelled by day and night over rugged country to meet requirements of [IRA] veterans on the run'.[32] A neighbour of Dan Mulvihill, Annie Cronin was treasurer of the local branch and attended first-aid classes conducted by the local doctor, Daniel Sheehan. She was involved in carrying dispatches and intelligence work in 1918–19 and with other members of the organisation, made haversacks and provided food for IRA members trying to evade the clutches of the police. She regularly hid ammunition – including a bomb – in a dugout near her home, which was often raided by the Black and Tans.[33]

The Keel Branch of Cumann na mBan, meanwhile, was particularly active and 'among the best of them' according to Dan Mulvihill.[34] The branch was established in 1917 by Fionán Lynch and Austin Stack with some eighty members joining in its first year.[35] Like their comrades in Milltown and elsewhere, its members regularly put their lives on the line. Mary Ann Duggan (*née* Dowd), for example, kept arms in her house. On one occasion, when Black and Tans arrived at her home at Laughtacalla, she distracted them while five IRA members sheltering there fled across the fields.[36] 'Many a time,' wrote John Heffernan of the Callinafercy IRA, 'when we called with our clothes wet she would leave her bed and stay up all night to have our clothes dry while we would have a few hours' sleep.'[37] Duggan's neighbour, Nora Corcoran, a teacher at nearby Castledrum National School, became Company Captain in June 1920 and 'devoted practically all her spare time to Vol. [Volunteer] and Cumann na mBan work'. Her sister Nellie Foley was also a member and their extensive list of duties and responsibilities including hosting first-aid lectures, fundraising, carrying messages, hiding weapons, sending parcels to prisoners, and catering for members of the IRA.[38] The Corcorans had a 'fully equipped dressing station' in their home at Boolteens for treating wounded Volunteers. From November 1920 they hid a dump of arms there and Corcoran acted as unofficial quartermaster supplying weapons and ammunition to Volunteers and collecting and storing the equipment after use. This activity had an additional danger as the Corcoran family lived just a stone's throw from the RIC barracks at Boolteens, although it had been abandoned by the summer of 1919.[39] Corcoran, described as 'a splendid organiser', also kept a close eye on enemy movements and hosted battalion meetings at her home.[40] 'Any time,' wrote

Bryan 'Bryannie' O'Brien of the Keel IRA, 'day or night, there was always an open door for them.'[41]

Mary 'May' O'Sullivan of Castledrum kept senior republicans like Pádraig Ó Siochfhradha (known by his pen name 'An Seabhac' and later a senator and chairman of Kerry County Council) during the 'Tan time' when 'Kerry was in a blaze.'[42] May's neighbour, Mary Dowd, meanwhile, handled and safeguarded arms at her home and collected and transported them for the IRA. She was instrumental in collecting the sum of £45 for the acquisition of guns and ammunition through the holding of concerts and *aerideacht* or cultural gatherings.[43] Dowd's home was located at the pier in Keel from where IRA members regularly crossed Castlemaine harbour by boat between Keel and Callinafercy to avoid police patrols on the main roads. In March 1921 Mary Dowd and her comrades in the Keel Cumann na mBan fed thirty men before they crossed by ferry from Keel to launch an assault on the Killorglin RIC.[44] In these and other fearless ways, the women of Cumann na mBan would play an integral and dangerous role in the lead-up to the attack on the Crown forces on 1 June 1921.

3

'TAKE UP THE CUDGEL … TO REMEDY THIS UNFORTUNATE VILLAGE'

'Milltown was at that time a deserted village with nobody left but the old and the very young.' So wrote an unidentified 'Milltowner' in an article about the Ballymacandy Ambush in *The Kerryman* newspaper, published in June 1971.[1] The author, local historian and writer of the 'Milltown Notes' in *The Kerryman* for many years, Denis Sugrue, was a schoolboy at the time of the incident, and was, fifty years later, recounting his memories of 1921. The portrayal of the village as one resembling that described in the Oliver Goldsmith poem was pertinent and is indicative of the economic stagnation at the time, which was compounded by the fatigue and fear in a community oppressed and terrified by the ongoing conflict between local republicans and the forces of the Crown. The village – a busy market town with thriving industries like tanning, malting and grinding corn throughout the nineteenth century – had been at the centre of local political turbulence on and off for decades. In many ways the trajectory of events in Milltown in the years before the War of Independence serve as a microcosm of developments nationally, replicating as they do the inexorable drift towards war in countless other towns and villages across Ireland.[2] Like all parts of Ireland, the locality endured the horrors of the Famine in the 1840s with two visiting clergymen from Wales recording that people living in the townland of Callinafercy were living 'more like animals than people'.[3] In the ten years between 1841 and 1851 the population of Milltown plummeted by almost 40 per cent.[4]

There were episodes of agrarian agitation in the wider Milltown area for decades, particularly after the Fenian Rising of 1867 and during the Land War. The first wife of senior Fenian and IRB leader Jeremiah O'Donovan-Rossa, Nora 'Nanno' Eager grew up at Ivy Lodge in Milltown and married O'Donovan-Rossa in 1853. Meetings in support of Daniel O'Connell's Repeal Campaign were held in the village in the early 1840s under the direction of Fr Batt O'Connor.[5] During the era of 'The Liberator', the village was often the setting for political rallies and meetings. O'Connell's meetings in Milltown as part of his campaign for Catholic Emancipation and civil rights are referred to in the correspondence of the Prendergast family of Bleach Road, Milltown in the 1840s.[6] Meetings opposing evictions were commonplace, particularly during the Land War when marching bands would lead rallies into the village. An example of the fiery rhetoric villagers heard in the 1880s was a speech from the MP for West Kerry, Edward Harrington, in which he decried the suppression of the Irish people: 'Why should they [the Irish people] be slaves to any land or to any nation, no matter how powerful … no land or no country where intelligent people, educated and right minded people exist should be without the right and without the principle of having a government of its own.'[7]

The new political organisations, which were formed around the country in the first two decades of the twentieth century, were replicated locally and would provide a fertile political breeding ground for the rebels of the Anglo-Irish War, many of them drawing members from among those who might have otherwise emigrated but for the impact of the First World War. Five months after the foundation of the Irish Volunteers at the Rotunda in Dublin, a Volunteer Company was formed in Milltown in March 1914, one of the first to be established in the county. The event was mentioned in the *Killarney Echo and South Kerry Chronicle* on 28 March 1914: 'I am also informed that at 4 p.m. on the same date and place in Milltown a Parish Volunteer Force will be organized. All the young blood and the old veterans are expected to attend. Drill instructors will be present. Up Kerry!'[8]

In October 1914 Tom O'Donnell, MP for West Kerry, who lived in Killorglin at the time, addressed a large gathering of Volunteers. He was led into the village by the Killorglin and Milltown companies, a marching band and the Killorglin Boy Scouts and presented bayonets to those assembled. The Volunteers then 'marched through the town, headed by the band, which played national airs, and back to the Square, where a large crowd had collected'.[9] Speaking in front of the gates to the Godfrey demesne, O'Donnell decried the 'yoke of landlordism'. A new Home Rule Bill was passed, he said, and would 'wipe away the stain of slavery under which we had lived for so long'.

Apart from the presence of the Volunteers, political agitation on behalf of tenants was commonplace and the Milltown Tenants' Association was active in campaigning for better living conditions for residents. Founded at the Crown Hotel in the village in November 1913, their aim was 'the improvement of our homes and to try and reduce the over-taxed rents we are trying to meet'. Its founding chairman, local creamery manager Thomas Godfrey, appealed to members to 'take up the cudgel and fight these rights as Irishmen and women, to look for such concessions, to remedy this unfortunate village, which has actually been a misery for upwards of a century'.[10] The First World War increased tension between nationalists and local loyalists. The walls of the bridge outside Glen Ellen, the home of Captain Creaghe-Howard, a Unionist Catholic, were defaced with the slogans 'Surrender Carson', 'Up Kerry', 'Home Rule' and a skull and crossbow.[11] Also, in May 1918, many local Protestants were raided for arms including the Batchelors and Reids in Callinafercy, the Blennerhassets and Wests of Kilderry and an attempt was made to seize weapons from Kilcoleman Abbey, home of the Godfrey family, and their relatives at nearby Callinafercy House.[12]

The general election of December 1918 and the subsequent establishment of the First Dáil on 21 January 1919, as well as the outbreak of the War of Independence on the same day, heralded a period of increased republican activity in Milltown and mid-Kerry. In the first week of January, for example, five local men were arrested for their involvement in an illegal assembly in the village on 24 November 1918. Over thirty men had marched under a flag bearing the initials 'I.R.' [Irish Republic]. Tom O'Connor, who would lead the attack at

Ballymacandy, along with Daniel Keane, Cornelius Corcoran, Denis Quirke and Patrick Flynn were arrested and brought before the courts but they declined to cooperate with the proceedings. Tom O'Connor refused to answer the charge as he did not recognise the court: 'Neither do I recognise the right of this, or any court constituted by a foreign power to try me.' O'Connor's defiance was met by 'loud cheers and stamping of feet' while Cornelius Corcoran shouted 'Three cheers for the Irish Republic?' Colonel Crane, presiding, sentenced them to three-months' hard labour in Cork jail.[13]

After Mass in Milltown on the following Sunday, a group bearing a banner with the words 'We demand the release of our prisoners' marched through the village.[14] In the same month, according to the *Killarney Echo and South Kerry Chronicle*, there was an increased police presence in Milltown: 'A force of military were brought into Milltown on Sunday. At night the police patrolled the streets and ordered the people off. This caused excitement which was further increased when the police drew the batons and attacked some young men.'[15] A police sergeant 'home on leave' was fired on in Callinafercy.[16] Elsewhere, the words 'England Out' were smeared on the walls opposite the Church of Ireland while the British coat of arms on the Crown Hotel was hacked off and the rubble strewn on the ground.[17] Milltown had a small but substantial Protestant community both in the village itself and spread throughout the surrounding parishes, who felt increasingly intimidated by these actions and which added to the general unease.

This rise in tenant activism as well as overt militant republicanism did not have a significant impact on the local gentry, the Godfreys of Kilcoleman Abbey although the family became more reclusive as the revolution progressed and as large country homes became an increasingly popular target for IRA attacks and searches by Black and Tans. In effect, as John Knightly has commented, 'the high stone walls built to keep the peasants out now served to keep the inhabitants in'.[18] With the outbreak of the war, and against a background of the wider national demise of the fortunes of the landed gentry, the Godfreys retained a positive relationship with villagers, many of whom kept animals on the family's demesne, and they continued to support social and charitable causes. Sir William Cecil Godfrey, the fifth baronet who inherited the heavily encumbered estate in 1900, remained a member of the Kerry Grand Jury and attended the Petty Sessions in Milltown but he did not really engage politically, being much more interested in hunting and shooting. It was under Sir William that most of the Godfrey estate was sold to its tenantry, one of the first in Kerry to be disposed of under the Wyndham Land Act of 1903.

During the War of Independence, the Godfrey mansion was raided for arms by local Volunteers but none were retrieved as Sir William had handed in his pistols to the local RIC for safekeeping at the end of 1919. IRA fugitives on the run would often hide in the safety of the dense woods of Kilcoleman and some were known to Sir William's wife, Lady Mary. Her niece, Mary Leeson Marshall, was robbed of her pony and trap, though it was later returned on the 'advice' of the local IRA captain.[19] The Leeson Marshalls' motorcar was stolen from outside Callinafercy House in 1920 and later found burnt out near Boolteens. Its owner, Major Leeson Marshall, had taken the precaution of removing the tyres from his vehicle in anticipation of theft but the IRA raiders succeeded in stealing it, remarking 'Sorry to have upset you, Major, but we must obey orders.'[20] The remarks suggest that despite a widespread marginalisation of the landed gentry and an increasing number of arson and violent attacks their properties, especially in south Kerry, the Godfreys and their relatives at Callinafercy House and the wider loyalist community were largely spared the worst excesses of IRA violence and were considered a benign rather than a hostile presence in the mid-Kerry community as the War of Independence raged.

Markham Richard Leeson Marshall is an important figure in the story of Ballymacandy not least because his meticulously maintained diaries and letters offer us a hugely valuable contemporaneous narrative of events at this time.[21] Born in 1857, he later served as a major in the Royal Munster Fusiliers until his retirement in 1918. He married Mabel, a daughter of Sir John F. Godfrey of Kilcoleman Abbey, in 1890 and the couple resided at Callinafercy House during their sojourns in Kerry when they were not resident in London. The modest mid-nineteenth-century dwelling would later have 'one of the great gardens of southern Ireland' and also featured a miniature children's playhouse known as the 'Doll's House' and which the Callinafercy Volunteers would use as a refuge during the War of Independence.[22] The major's sister, Edith, Lady Gordon, lived at Ard na Sídhe overlooking Caragh Lake and wrote a memoir, *The Winds of Time*, which describes the turbulent times – she was a supporter of Home Rule, which caused some bemusement in the wider family. His other sister, Mary was married to Sir William Godfrey. The major's first wife, Mabel, died two years after their marriage and barely a year after the birth of their daughter, May.[23] The major remarried in 1906 and with his new wife, Meriel Hodson, continued to reside at Callinafercy until 1939.

The family's influence is described by Callinafercy historian Patrick V. O'Sullivan in his memoir, *I Heard the Wild Birds Sing*. He recalls that children attending garden parties at Callinafercy House 'were constantly reminded of the blessings bestowed upon Ireland by the royal family across the Irish sea'.[24] The major, while loyalist in outlook, had mixed views, however, about Home Rule and British governance in Ireland – he often corresponded on such matters with the local MP, Tom O'Donnell. Despite an innate loyalism, the major was a realist who usually knew the direction of the prevailing political winds.[25]

The Royal Irish Constabulary in Milltown was based in a barracks at the corner of Main Street and the Castlemaine road in a large, three-storey building, which later became Lombard's Hotel and Cosgrove's public house. There was no barracks in Castlemaine at this time and the nearest police bases were Killorglin, about four miles away, and Boolteens in Keel, about five miles away, but the latter post was abandoned by the police after the barracks was burnt out by the IRA in July 1919.[26] By 1919 there were 'five to ten men' stationed in Milltown and their sergeant, William Whinton, was considered 'a decent type' by one local IRA member, James Cronin.[27] In his history of the locality, Denis Sugrue recalls how some of the RIC families were part and parcel of village life:

> The police barrack had an attraction, all of its own, for the younger generation. Perhaps it was because a married

man with a school-going family always occupied the living quarters. This gave the Monastery [school] boys and the Convent [school] girls, too, a kind of liaison with the policeman's children. Two, and sometimes, three, other families of the resident constables lived out with their families in Church Street.[28]

Activities at the barracks were the focus of much chatter in the village at least once a month when the local district inspector would arrive to put his men through their paces:

Once a month, the District Inspector, or better known as the DI, visited the barracks. It usually happened on a Saturday, and, being a free day from school, the lads congregated outside the barrack-yard gate to be intrigued by the target practice that usually concluded the Inspector's visit. The 'bull's eye' was at the inside of the yard, and only recently, when demolition of the old walls took place, some of the leaden slugs were found embedded in the mortar portions of the target wall.[29]

As the war escalated in the summer of 1920, a controversial visit by a senior army officer to the RIC Barracks in Milltown had a profound impact on the police there and created repercussions that lasted through to the summer of the following year. Gerald Bryce Ferguson Smyth was appointed RIC Divisional Commissioner for Munster in May 1920. On his appointment to the divisional role, Smyth, a decorated soldier during the Great War, set about dealing with the IRA with ruthless determination. He 'issued bombastic and radical instructions, ostensibly to boost police morale, for the suppression of an intensified IRA campaign'.[30] He made a series of visits to barracks in Kerry in June 1920 aimed at motivating the police to take the fight to the IRA. The background to Smyth's controversial visit to Milltown was the so-called 'Listowel Mutiny'. The RIC in Listowel had been ordered to vacate their barracks to accommodate British military. When the officers refused to do so, Smyth arrived a few days later and told his men that martial law was about to be declared in Ireland and, whether they liked it or not, they were being transferred to other rural stations while the military would take over the larger towns. There would be a new more aggressive policy towards the rebels: hunger-strikers would be allowed to die, no more inquests would be held and Sinn Féin would be 'wiped out' with the arrival of reinforcements. Most controversially, he ordered:

> … when civilians are seen approaching, shout 'hands up.' Should the order not be immediately obeyed, shoot, and shoot with effect … The more you shoot, the better I will like you, and I assure you that no policeman will get into trouble for shooting any man.[31]

Smyth's instructions, which were redolent of the 'shoot to kill' policy during the Troubles in Northern Ireland decades later, led to a revolt among the local constabulary, prompted by the response of Constable Jeremiah Mee, who pulled off his belt and bayonet and threw them on the table saying, '… to hell with you, you murderer'.[32] Mee and several of his colleagues revolted and resigned from the police.

Commander Smyth arrived in Milltown the following day, Sunday 20 June, to rally his troops and relay the new instructions. He was accompanied by the County Inspector of the RIC, John Marcus Poer O'Shee.[33] Fifty-one-year-old O'Shee, a native of Dublin, was just five days into his new role as County Inspector for Kerry.[34] Greeting Smyth on his arrival at Milltown Barracks were Sergeant James Collery and seven constables: Peter O'Toole, Patrick Brannock, John Curtin, John Quirke, James Lynch, Cornelius McCarthy and Edward Reilly.[35] Smyth placed his gun on the table, telling the men he was answerable to no man in Ireland but the Prime Minister, David Lloyd George. The RIC, he said, had been on the back foot in their battle with the IRA but radical steps were being taken to reverse that trend. The police needed to be more assertive and more organised, he said, reiterating the command that officers should 'not hesitate to shoot' regardless of the circumstances.[36]

The majority of the officers listening to Smyth took his visit with a pinch of salt and treated his instructions as 'one of the "comings and goings" of highly placed officers' but Constable Peter O'Toole took a very different view. He told Smyth and O'Shee that when he had joined the Royal Irish Constabulary, he didn't anticipate having to shoot anybody. Smyth 'made little' of this argument, telling O'Toole that times had changed and tactics needed to change too. He accused the constable of 'cowardice' and departed the barracks. Constable O'Toole's insubordination was punished a few days later. He was notified that he was being transferred to Rathmore on the Kerry–Cork border. But O'Toole refused to relocate from Milltown. On 29 June County Inspector O'Shee was forced to return to the barracks at Milltown with two lorry-loads of RIC men armed with bombs and rifles. He spoke to O'Toole:

> in a fatherly way and asked him why he would not take his transfer. 'Well, if you want to know,' came the reply, 'I did not join the police to lead around Black and Tans and the scum of England which have been brought into the force.' The officer [O'Shee] tried to soften his subordinate and drew a picture of his bright prospects in the force, at the same time pointing out that such an attitude as he (the policeman) was taking would create disaffection among the other men.[37]

After pleading with O'Toole for two hours, the County Inspector told him he would have to be suspended from the RIC. 'Take that and that,' replied O'Toole, throwing his jacket, belt and revolver onto the table. The ex-constable went to Killarney 'where he was well known'.[38] A month later O'Toole's adversary, Commissioner Smyth, was assassinated by the IRA in the smoking room of the County Club in Cork city on 17 July 1921.[39]

Shortly after Smyth's controversial visit, in July 1920 the RIC in Milltown decided to vacate their barracks and relocated to a large three-storey property on Main Street in the centre of the village. The new base for the Milltown RIC had until recently been occupied by Dr Daniel Sheehan, who was the local doctor and also medical officer for the local IRA brigade. Sheehan, who ran his medical practice from the house (as had his father-in-law, Dr James Hanafin) moved to a new home at

Glen Ellen on the outskirts of the village. The reason for the RIC move is not entirely clear but a report in the *Killarney Echo and South Kerry Chronicle* suggests that the new headquarters 'commands a better strategic position than the old one which was a corner building at the end of the street'.[40] The installation of communications equipment at the new barracks was almost scuppered by a bold attack by the IRA. Members of the Farmers' Bridge Company of the Kerry No.1 Brigade attempted to ambush the RIC communications team on their way to Milltown to install a wireless station. One trench had been dug in the road by the time the police passed through and they 'actually passed over the hole that had been made in the road'. The police vehicle proceeded unhindered to Milltown from where the RIC communicated with Tralee.[41]

Shortly after the abandonment of the former barracks located opposite the entrance to the Godfrey demesne, it was attacked by the IRA on 10 August in an operation led by Dan Mulvihill of Brackhill, which included brothers Dan and Patrick Allman from Rockfield and brothers Charlie and Tom Daly of Knockaneacoulteen.[42] It is assumed this was the cause of the abandonment of the new police headquarters – in October 1920 the RIC left Milltown completely and withdrew to neighbouring larger barracks, including Killorglin.[43] This was not an unusual phenomenon: in the same month as the old Milltown barracks was attacked, the barracks in Kilgarvan and Portmagee were also evacuated.[44] As the war against the RIC, the Black and Tans and the Auxiliaries intensified during 1920 and barracks in isolated, rural areas became increasingly vulnerable, the relative security offered by more fortified structures in the larger towns became essential. In Glenbeigh, for example, the IRA 'flaked away at the barracks there and we wounded a few. We had them confined to their barracks,' said Bertie Scully of Glencar, 'and we controlled 20 X 15 square miles in which they could not move.'[45] The *Atlas of the Irish Revolution* maps the closure of 700 of the barracks, which had been used at the start of 1919, as being closed by the beginning of 1921, 'geographically illustrating the shrinkage of British authority and control.'[46] By the end of 1920 James Collery, by then living in his own home in the Square in Milltown with his wife and a young and growing family, found himself having to travel four miles to and from his new base in Killorglin every day rather than the short walk he had previously enjoyed along the street to his workplace.

Milltown in the autumn of 1920 was a grim place. Economic and commercial activity was restricted, employment was scarce, social occasions and interaction restrained. Fear, anxiety and paranoia pervaded the community. Local memory holds that when a police curfew was imposed from eight o'clock in the evening, it was a requirement that a list of occupants be written and maintained on the back of the door of each home so that it could be inspected by the police in search of those on the run. Suspicious responses would see men and women corralled in the Square for questioning. The intensification of policing methods led to more viciousness against ordinary civilians. In September the *Kerry People* reported that 'a young man in the Milltown district was tarred and a young lady a short time previous had her hair cut.'[47] On 9 October it reported 'a labourer recently tarred in the Milltown district has been taken away by the Crown forces.'[48] Tarring and cropping of hair were used to intimidate and publicly scar and shame victims and in recent years, the cropping of women's hair, often accompanied by sexual assault, has come to be acknowledged as a sinister feature of the tit-for-tat conflict between the IRA and their enemies.[49] With such random violence being inflicted on the civilian population, the County Inspector of the RIC, writing in October 1920, appeared to be relying more on hope than reality when he noted that there seemed to be indications that 'the murder gang is finding it more difficult to draw the whole body [of the people] with them in their schemes'.[50] If anything, the direct opposite was the case. An oppressed and distressed civilian population had become increasingly fearful and disillusioned and were looking for support and protection. Against the backdrop of a seemingly endless and spiralling descent into a new, more vicious and bitter phase of the war, the men of the mid-Kerry IRA plotted and prepared to seek their revenge.

4

'FAIRYLAND'

The motives of the men and women who took up arms and laid ambush against the representatives of King and Empire a century ago were inspired by many things: a love of Irish language and culture, an ambition to finally settle the land question, a sense of injustice after centuries of occupation, a hatred of British rule in their homeland, an attempt to settle old scores and personal grievances, or a combination of these and many other factors. For Dan Mulvihill, a romantic attachment to and a love of the unspoiled landscape that surrounded him is a constant theme in his dramatic tales of the time.

By the autumn of 1920 Mulvihill and his comrades had withdrawn to the relative safety and seclusion of the rugged and remote parish of Glencar, deep in the foothills of the towering MacGillycuddy's Reeks mountains and about as far as they could get from the police and the dreaded Black and Tans. The RIC had abandoned their barracks in Glencar in June 1920 following an ambush by the IRA, and within a few weeks it had become 'a small Republic'.[1] By this time, Mulvihill and his peers were on the run from the authorities but they were also regrouping to train and plan for further attacks on the enemy.

His romantic descriptions of the county are vividly juxtaposed against the bloodshed and violence that then prevailed:

> I had seen a lot of beautiful places in the world, mostly tropical, but I had never seen anything to touch Glencar as it was at this time. From the top of the parish to the hotel at the foot of Caragh Lake was one riot of colour. It was the most beautiful place I had ever seen. All the trees were deciduous, and the tints of Autumn made a Fairyland of it all … We had Carrauntoohil, at its foot Derrynafeena, and two famous passes, Bealach Béama and Bealach Oisín … it was grand to be young, and on the run in Glencar that winter [in] 1920.[2]

Mulvihill was among a large number of his peers who now formed small units known as 'Flying Columns' and 'Active Service Units'. The first were 'full-time and roamed about', launching surprise attacks on the enemy, while the latter were 'similar guerrilla bands that remained local and part-time, coming out primarily to support the operations of the former although they also conducted operations on their own or with the support of the rank and file of their brigades'.[3] The Flying Columns, wrote IRA Volunteer Jeremiah Murphy, 'had been brought to some degree of efficient fighting units. No longer were they a bunch of frightened men trying to evade arrest. They had all seen some action during the course of barracks attacks.'[4] But the Flying Column achieved more in reputation than reality. Historian John Borgonovo suggests that the columns were few in number and inflicted a small number of casualties but their 'audaciousness in the face of overwhelming

British superiority raised republican morale and helped create the myth of the Flying Column'.[5] In the case of the Milltown and neighbouring companies at this time, the Flying Column was led by John 'Jack' Flynn as commanding officer, Dan Mulvihill as adjutant, and their neighbour from Brackhill, Jimmy Cronin.[6] Amid the mountain mists and rocky valleys of Glencar, they trained, drilled, made shot for their weapons and prepared to engage with the enemy once more.

Towards the end of 1920 two ambushes, which occurred within hours of each other just a few miles from Ballymacandy, had deep and grave consequences for those on both sides of the conflict and reverberated all the way through to the events of 1 June 1921. They came in the context of a general order from IRA headquarters to battalions around the country that 'all the Tans were to be shot on sight'.[7] On the night of 31 October 1920 at about 10 p.m., and acting on tip-offs from local members of Cumann na mBan, members of the Listry and Callinafercy IRA, as well as Con Lucey, captain of the Caragh Lake company, confronted two Black and Tans at Hillville on the Milltown road near Killorglin.[8] They had taken up positions on either side of the road. Daniel Healy, the Listry Company lieutenant provided a graphic account of the incident:

> Dan Allman [Rockfield] and our group took up position behind the bank on the side of the road. The two Tans came along on cycles and, acting on orders, one of our party called upon them to halt. They ignored the call and attempted to cycle through. Our party had orders to fire on the Tans if they failed to halt. We opened fire. One Tan

went down. He was killed outright. The second Tan was wounded but he tried to go on. After travelling about 10 yards the wounded Tan fell against the ditch. Daniel Allman went out on the road and took some of the party with him. He approached the wounded Tan and brought him to the spot where the dead Tan lay. Dan Allman questioned the wounded Tan, who pleaded for a chance. He said he would resign [from the police] next morning. Dan Allman reminded him that he was a Tan. The Tan again pleaded that he was the only son of a widow. Near the side of the road where this was taking place some members of the Killorglin Company had been 'standing to' in a hayshed and one them came out to see what was happening on the road … Daniel Allman invited this man to finish off the wounded Tan, but he declined the invitation. Dan Allman then called on us to finish off the Tan.[9]

According to another version of events, members of the Callinafercy Company, who knew that the Tans were seeing two local girls, wanted only to disarm rather than kill them. It is understood that the man 'invited' by Allman to kill one of the officers was Ned Langford of the Callinafercy Company. When he refused to do so, Allman threatened to kill him and Langford's company captain, John Heffernan was forced to intervene. Heffernan also intervened to prevent the two local women being tarred by the IRA – a vicious punishment used to intimidate and admonish women for 'company keeping' with the enemy.

On hearing the shooting, Constable Patrick Foley from Killorglin RIC Barracks cycled towards the scene. He discovered 22-year-old Constable John Herbert Evans and 24-year-old Albert Caseley lying dead on the road. Evans was 'lying on his face and Constable Caseley on his back, both still bleeding profusely and bearing marks of having been fired at close range'.[10] Evans, from Belfast and Caseley, from Brixton Hill in London were both soldiers during the First World War. The constables' names were read into the record of the House of Commons by the Chief Secretary for Ireland, Sir Hamar Greenwood, in his weekly list of casualties. Speaking of Constable Caseley, he told MPs:

> He was riding his bicycle, and was shot through the back of the head and killed – a man who had served his country for four years in Persia and Mesopotamia, and who went to Ireland at the call of the British Government to serve the country there; who was the main support of a widowed mother – a working-class mother living here in London. I think it ought to bring home vividly to this House the realities of the situation.[11]

The *Cork Examiner* meanwhile reported that Constable Patrick Foley, who was the first on the scene, had been authorised to provide his account of the finding of the bodies to the Press Association. In his account he claimed that the 'majority of the people disassociated themselves entirely from the crime and expressed their disgust with the whole thing and tendered their sympathies'.[12] Foley also made the unsubstantiated and fanciful claim to have discussed the incident with Prime Minister David Lloyd George, who he claimed 'congratulated him very warmly on his distinguished career in the army, and enquired closely into the details of the discovery [of the bodies]'.[13] There is no evidence to suggest that a lowly RIC constable in Killorglin was in any form of communication with the prime minister about an incident that was by no means unique in Ireland in 1920, but Foley's self-indulgent comments and public statements in the press about the deaths of his colleagues made him a visible and prime target for his adversaries in the IRA. He was referred to as 'a bad peeler' [policeman] by Gregory Ashe, the brother of Thomas Ashe and a member of the Lispole Company of the Kerry No.1 Brigade.[14] Raising his head above the parapet was a bold and naive act on the part of Constable Foley in the maelstrom of the conflict in mid-Kerry in the autumn of 1920. From that time onwards, according to Kerry No.1 Brigade member Billy Mullins, Foley was 'badly wanted' by the Irish Republican Army.[15]

Reprisal and retaliation for the murders at Hillville was swift. After the RIC in Killorglin retrieved the bodies of Constables Caseley and Evans in the early hours of the following morning, 1 November, they proceeded to 'shoot up the town'. The Sinn Féin Hall at Lower Bridge Street as well as a garage, timber mill, the creamery and other buildings including the rooms of the Total Abstinence Society (and all of the musical instruments of its band) were burned.[16] Shops and houses were forcibly entered and many families fled the town.[17] The *Irish Independent* reported that: 'Mr DM O'Sullivan, The Square, was taken from his house and shot, receiving four wounds, that in the stomach being most serious … Many houses were visited, but the "wanted" men were not at home. Shop doors and windows were broken in.'[18] Also targeted was the home of Fionán Mac Coluim, a prominent Irish-language activist and campaigner who was Chief Organiser and *Ard Timire* of the Gaelic League in Kerry.[19] Major Leeson Marshall wrote in a letter to his daughter:

> Killorglin was like a city of the dead, all houses shuttered up, not a soul to be seen but two or three people running for the train to get out of the place for the night. Foley's garage smouldering ruins and when we got to Hillville a pool of blood that nearly made me sick, a horrible sight I shall never forget. One reads of these things but when one sees them! They [Caseley and Evans] were biking back unarmed from Milltown direction on Sunday night and were waylaid just where one slows down. Not being in at roll call, a constable biked out to look for them and it is said nearly went mad at the site. Foley's and a teacher's house burned, and Mrs. O'Donovan's son 'Dr' Dinny O got a bullet in him, how I do not know.[20]

He later noted in his diary the compensation that would be levied on local ratepayers for the damage sustained during the Black and Tans' retaliatory rampage in Killorglin, including the compensation sought for the deaths of Constables Caseley and Evans:

2 Policemen shot	£3,500
Stephens' Mill burned	£9,000
Foley's garage	£5,000
Teacher's residence	£700
Young men's SF (club)	£270
	£18,470

'A specimen,' Leeson Marshall concluded 'of the loss in blood & wealth the country is suffering.'[21] It was a sentiment shared by his brother-in-law, Sir William Godfrey, who wrote, 'there will be a garnishee order on my demesne for this [the burnings]. Damn good job if it is taken – I'm done.'[22]

The Crown forces also turned their attention to Milltown in retaliation for the deaths at Hillville, in the knowledge that the attack had been instigated by the IRA companies in the neighbouring districts of Listry and Callinafercy. Just hours after the incident, a group of Black and Tans and Auxiliaries arrived in the village on the morning of 1 November, because according to Tom O'Connor, 'they had an order that fellows had come from there who had done the [Hillville] job.'[23] Shots were fired indiscriminately on the streets forcing many residents, particularly women and children, to flee to the supposed safety of Kilcoleman Abbey where Mary, Lady Godfrey, provided blankets and cups of tea. Other residents barricaded themselves in the post office.[24] Some took refuge in the Catholic church and were followed there by the militia.[25] Challenged by parish priest, Fr Patrick Buckley – who called them murderers and looters – to leave the House of God, they did so. The parish clerk, Jack O'Shea, was wounded and hay owned by a man named Con Slattery was set alight. The Slattery home at Lyre Road was set ablaze and Margaret Slattery, a member of Cumann na mBan, was taken to the military barracks in Tralee and was court-martialled a few days later in the Technical School in Tralee though the charges put to her are not recorded. She claimed that Major Mackinnon ripped the rosary beads she was wearing from around her neck.[26] Father Alexander 'Sandy' O'Sullivan, then a curate in Milltown, intervened with the authorities on her behalf and she was released.

As their colleagues were terrorising the people of Milltown, a number of RIC and Black and Tans raided local homes for arms. Amelia Mason of Cumann na mBan was at her home at Brackhill and had heard about the ambush at Hillville the previous night. Raids on the home she shared with her husband, Alexander 'Sonny' Mason, leader of the Kiltallagh IRA, were commonplace as it was a suspected hiding place for IRA arms. Amelia Mason pre-empted the arrival of the Black and Tans on 1 November by removing and hiding elsewhere as many of those arms as she could. She later recounted what followed:

> House was raided that night after ambush at Hillville by Tans – there were arms still in dump in house which were not found. I had to remove these day after. The Tans who were firing shots all during night after ambush wounded a man who refused drink – myself and a neighbour removed him from street when firing seized to a place of safety. I administered first aid till Dr. arrived and nursed him after. The next day I was ordered from town by RIC and was not allowed back for two weeks.[27]

The morning visit of the police and Tans from Killorglin was just the beginning of the retaliatory reaction of the authorities. Tom O'Connor of the local IRA recalled that the patrol which came to the village that morning 'said that they would come back that night to burn Milltown'.[28] In anticipation of such an assault on the village later that night, over thirty Volunteers were quickly mobilised to lie in wait for the return of the Black and Tans. O'Connor rounded up his men and the ambushers hunkered down in the dark at the ringfort of Fort Agnes (Poll na Ratha) adjacent to Kilderry Wood on the Milltown to Killorglin road, a position which offered good elevation overlooking the main road.[29] The IRA perch was also just a short distance from the ruins of the thirteenth-century Augustinian Abbey of Our Lady of Bello Loco at Killagha. The once prosperous priory was situated not far from the early medieval site where St Colman founded his monastery and from which the parish of Kilcoleman (nowadays Milltown parish) derived its name.[30] Centuries before the Black and Tans went on a rampage of burnings, it was the armies of Oliver Cromwell who had reputedly burned and destroyed much of the abbey during the Confederate Wars.[31] The IRA men gathered in the dark in the thicket on 1 November 1920 made no distinction between the Cromwellian terror of the seventeenth century and the Black and Tans' campaign of the twentieth – there was a continuum of suppression and occupation by a foreign enemy, which they were fighting to destroy.

The group assembled at 9.30 p.m. and Dan Mulvihill states they were armed with shotguns and revolvers and lay in ambush despite only having 'enough cartridges for one volley'.[32] A Crossley Tender carrying a party of RIC and Black and Tans passed at about 1.30 a.m. The lorry came under heavy fire and hit the ditch but reversed onto the road again and drove away from Milltown on a byroad. It is believed that three or four Tans were injured by which time their assailants had to abandon the attack for lack of ammunition. The IRA attack meant that Milltown itself escaped the planned reprisal but the police who escaped with their lives were still intent on wreaking revenge.

While the ambush was under way at Kilderry Wood, the Listry Company under Dan Allman, also expecting retaliation in their area for the deaths at Hillville, lay in wait at Ballymalis Cross on the Killorglin to Killarney road, expecting the Black and Tans to travel to Listry via the main road. Unbeknown to Allman and his men, the lorry had instead travelled towards Milltown. The lorry drove off from Kilderry and away from Milltown and headed instead in the direction of Listry via Bleach Road through Lyre and Ballyvirrane.[33] When they arrived at their destination, Listry Creamery experienced the wrath of the Black and Tans, who set it ablaze.[34] The burning of Listry Creamery was an example of a tactic increasingly employed by the Black and Tans and it was one of eight destroyed by Crown forces in Kerry in 1920–21.[35] The burning of creameries was not only a means of disabling local milk production and agricultural activity, it was a symbolic and highly visible warning to the IRA that arson would be used in reprisals for ambushes and attacks. It also 'undid the fruits of over a decade of British land reform in Ireland which since 1908 had subsidised farmers to buy their own land. Nothing could have provoked quite so much loathing for the Crown forces.'[36] In May 1921 Messrs Watson's Creamery in Killorglin was burned and creameries in Kilflynn and Lixnaw in north Kerry were shut down.[37] It was a strategy for which the Chief Secretary for Ireland was unapologetic: 'these measures are not taken against specific individuals but are intended to bring home to the inhabitants of the locality generally their responsibility for outrages committed with their knowledge and connivance'.[38]

The incidents at Hillville and Kilderry occurred during one of the most violent and turbulent weeks of the War of Independence, at a time when it seemed that the conflict was spiralling out of control. On the day of the Kilderry ambush, 1 November 1920, eighteen-year-old medical student Kevin Barry was hanged at Mountjoy jail in Dublin for his role in the deaths of three policemen. The previous day, the funeral had taken place of the Lord Mayor of Cork, Terence MacSwiney, who had died on hunger strike on 25 October. These events attracted international attention as well as outrage and condemnation of British policy in Ireland. The ambushes in mid-Kerry also coincided with the beginning of one of the most significant events in the history of the conflict in Kerry; the so-called week-long 'Siege of Tralee' during which the town was effectively cut off from the outside world, terrifying local civilians. The events were reported in newspapers across the globe.

One of the major consequences of events in Tralee was the retreat of many senior IRA members from the town to the safety of the countryside. During January and February 1921, Tralee continued to be a hostile place for IRA members trying to evade the authorities. On 28 January, for example, there had been a major 'round-up' of IRA suspects with many Tralee members taken into custody.[39] Many of these men would retreat to the hills and mountains of west Kerry and, eventually, to a new temporary headquarters in Keel on the Dingle Peninsula. It would be from there that many of those who engaged the enemy at Ballymacandy would set out on a summer's morning in June 1921.

5

'OUR STATE GETS WORSE'

As the men of the mid-Kerry IRA wintered in Glencar, the New Year's editorial in the *Kerry People* at the beginning of 1921 noted that the return of Éamon de Valera from his tour of America 'has once more produced peace whisperings in many quarters' but added that 'we cannot discern anything tangible in them'.[1] However, the political situation in Ireland and in Kerry as 1921 dawned remained extremely febrile. And while there may have been talk of peace, the IRA war continued unabated. 'It was,' recalled Ned Horan of the Firies IRA, 'very hot all during '21'.[2] Fifty-nine police and nine soldiers were killed in Ireland in first two months of the year.[3] Shootings, ambushes, kidnappings, burnings and reprisals escalated across the country in their ferocity as well as in numbers. But the IRA in Kerry continued to be stymied by a lack of weapons and an incoherence in their war plan.[4] Sinéad Joy contends that in the first six months of 1921, the Kerry IRA limited its activity to the 'comparatively safe practices of raiding, road-trenching and mail robbery'.[5] These activities were not without consequences for civilians and posed significant disruption to normal commercial, social and economic activity. The extent of this disturbance in the mid-Kerry area in the early months of 1921 is evident in extracts from the diaries of Major Leeson Marshall of Callinafercy:

> *27 February – Sunday* – Road trenched again & trees felled across that Kilderry Wood. M [his wife, Meriel] did not go to church. I took pony through Abbey road.

> *5 April – Tuesday* – No post. Went to Killorglin to inquire. Hear the authorities have closed the line from Tralee to Mallow so our train runs idle to Farranfore junction. Post men warned their service no longer required. Our state gets worse. Hear no flour in Killarney. I got 5st as a precaution. Heard railway closed on a/c of 1st, Headford ambush, 2nd, Millstreet bridge blown up.

> *27 April – Wednesday* – Roads blocked at Milltown by felling trees & trench said to be 20ft wide cut across Killorglin to Killarney road at Ballymalis & one 12 ft. wide across Milltown to Killarney one.[6]

These incidents occurred against a descent into a general state of lawlessness and unrest. The monthly reports prepared by County RIC Inspectors detailed the extent of the task facing those charged with the enforcement of law and order. In April and May alone, for example, the RIC in Kerry recorded 225 'outrages' ranging from murder to robbery and arson to malicious injury.[7]

The peaceful 'paradise' of Dan Mulvihill's adopted home of Glencar was shattered at the end of February 1921 in a shooting that had dramatic consequences, which reverberated right through to the ambush at Ballymacandy. The town of Killorglin, district headquarters for the RIC, was the focus of much of the local IRA activity in the spring of 1921 and the Crown Forces based there became increasingly vulnerable to attack. Despite the fact that the town was home to the largest barracks of the RIC in mid-Kerry, Killorglin, according to many of the sources, was not home to a particularly active IRA company nor was there, says Tom O'Connor, the same level of popular support for the Volunteers as there was in other parts of Kerry.[8] Bertie Scully of the Glencar IRA charged that they could get little information from informants in the town and that the 'Killorglin town crowd were no good'.[9] Part of the reason for this may have been the towering presence and influence of Tom O'Donnell, the Irish Parliamentary Party MP for West Kerry from 1900 to 1918 who lived at Lower Bridge Street until 1921. He was a vocal opponent of the IRA and his influence in Killorglin made its population 'at best, apathetic to the Irish Volunteers and there was no great support for the Republicans in the town during the Tan War and Civil War'.[10] Killorglin, the largest town and centre of economic activity in mid-Kerry, had followed the trajectory of most other towns in the growing cultural, political and armed revolutions. A branch of Sinn Féin was set up in December 1907 and the Gaelic League had a strong presence in the town since 1901.[11] At the annual Puck Fair of 1908, a large banner bearing the words 'Sinn Féin, Sinn Féin Amháin' (Ourselves, Ourselves Alone) was hung in the town. The iconic fair – dating from the early 1600s – was banned by the authorities in 1920 – perhaps because 'S.F. [Sinn Féin] Volunteers' were among the organisers – but went ahead regardless and a tricolour flown from the platform was taken down by the RIC before being replaced by another hastily-stitched flag.[12]

The Killorglin garrison was firmly in the sights of the local IRA at the end of 1920. The local battalions were planning an attack on a police patrol: this particular patrol left the barracks in the town most nights, travelling across the Laune Bridge then turning left towards Milltown and Castlemaine before returning to base. Its regularity made it an obvious target. The ambush was set for Saturday 26 February and included members of the Milltown, Callinafercy and Glencar companies of the 6th Battalion. The Glencar men left their homes on foot the previous night, crossing the River Laune at a ford at Dungeel and slept for most of the day in a hayshed near Milltown. There they received the sacrament of confession from Fr Alexander 'Sandy' O'Sullivan, the curate in Milltown.[13] The ambushers took up their position later that night at a spot opposite the Laune Bridge on the Milltown road, but after several hours, the RIC patrol was nowhere to be seen. Jimmy Cronin and Dan Mulvihill went to investigate and learned that they had taken a different route, travelling instead towards Glencar via Langford Street.[14] Poor scouting was blamed, and the ambush party packed up to go home.[15]

Among the party were two members of the Glencar Company, Paddy Murphy and Joe Taylor. Taylor was Officer Commanding of the Glencar Company.[16] On returning to his home at Lyranes in rural Glencar, he fell asleep. The police who had travelled out from Killorglin, entered and brought him to where they had taken others into custody. Taylor was shot in the thigh and haemorrhaging badly when, according to Bertie Scully, one officer attempted first aid but soon fled.[17] Dan Mulvihill later heard the police officers 'kept the local women back until he bled to death'[18] but Taylor did receive medical treatment from a local doctor.[19] It was to no avail: he died within the hour. Among the patrol of RIC and Black and Tans was Constable Joseph Cooney, who it was claimed 'pulled Joe out of his house the morning he was killed'.[20] Shortly after the incident, the RIC decided their barracks in Glencar was no longer safe and it was abandoned. Along with Joseph Cooney – another of the local constables who withdrew from the rural barracks and took up duties in Killorglin – was James Collery. Cooney, Collery and their colleagues, it was alleged, were 'very bitter at having to leave Glencar'.[21] Their involvement in Joe Taylor's death would have deadly consequences for Cooney and Collery in the months that followed.

IRA engagements with the forces of the Crown continued to increase in frequency and intensity in mid-Kerry and across the county in the weeks and months before Ballymacandy. A fortnight after Joe Taylor died, an attempt was made on the life of Head Constable Blake of Killorglin RIC. Five men – Dan Mulvihill, James Cronin, Jack Flynn, Tom O'Connor and Denis Quirke – entered Blake's home. Blake was sitting at the kitchen table 'but he had a child in his arms', and this saved his life.[22] Four days later, up to thirty IRA members attempted to attack a police party returning to their barracks at the Square in Killorglin. They set themselves up in the front rooms of some of the houses near the barracks with the occupants being 'politely but firmly' ordered into their back rooms.[23] From the houses, the attackers began to shoot at a patrol. 'We knew that we couldn't take the barracks,' said Tom O'Connor, the officer in command, 'but the idea was to give mostly the men experience!'[24] The incident represented an increasing confidence among the IRA rank and file who 'marched from the town at an early hour, having suffered no casualties.'[25]

Meanwhile, the ambush of soldiers at Headford Junction in east Kerry on 21 March – the 'biggest ambush of its kind in Ireland' – represented the highest death toll during a single incident in the War of Independence in Kerry.[26] The ambush claimed the life of Dan Allman of Rockfield. His mortuary card, featuring an image of Allman in his IRA cap and bandolier would become as identifiable and synonymous with the conflict as the police 'Wanted' poster for Tipperary's Dan Breen. As the incident at Headford was underway, a Flying Column under Paddy Cahill attempted to ambush a police patrol at Lispole near Dingle, but the IRA lost three men – Thomas Ashe, Tommy Hawley and Maurice Fitzgerald – during the incident. A month later, members of the mid-Kerry companies were involved in an attack at Glenbeigh railway station during which police were fired upon and the IRA accumulated a large cache of weapons and ammunition.[27] The IRA companies represented include those from Tralee who were based in a hideout in the mountains near Keel as well as members from Castlegregory, Dingle, Inch, Annascaul, Camp and Glencar, all under the command of Tom O'Connor of Milltown and Tadhg Brosnan of Castlegregory.[28] The official report on the incident noted that the 'rebels numbered from 25 to 35' and that 'a Lewis gun and five rifles were captured from the military'.[29] In response to the incident, the authorities imposed a blockade and clamped down on the rebels in the Kerry No.3 Brigade area in south

Kerry, which was reported to be 'in a state of crisis and on the brink of starvation' in May 1921.[30]

The violence in Kerry during the month of May continued in a vicious circle of tit-for-tat attacks, injuries and deaths. Two RIC head constables were killed, William Storey in Castleisland on 8 May and Francis Benson in Tralee the following week.[31] Eight policemen, including Auxiliaries, died in an ambush on the Bog Road near Rathmore on 4 May in a joint operation involving members of the Kerry No.2 and Cork No.2 brigades. The RIC had been responding to reports that a Thomas Sullivan – labelled a spy and an informer by the IRA – had been murdered and his body dumped on the road. The RIC described Sullivan as a 'harmless ballad singer' whose body was placed 'to bait a trap for the police'.[32] Burnings, round-ups and reprisals against IRA members and civilians took place in Kenmare, Cahersiveen and Farranfore. On 9 May at Ballykissane, near Killorglin, two police were fired upon.[33] According to Edward Langford of the Callinafercy Company who was involved in the attack, the IRA ammunition used in the incident left a lot to be desired; 'our stuff was useless' as it was 'our own filling'.[34] One of the Black and Tans fell off his bicycle and fled the scene on foot and the other cycled away to the barracks to alert his colleagues.

In the seven days before the ambush at Ballymacandy, the casualty list among the Crown Forces around Ireland was high. On 23 May Constable Joseph Maguire was shot dead during an ambush in Lower Shirdagh, County Mayo. His assailants were 'pursued by the RIC for 8 miles through bogs and over hills [and] one wounded rebel was picked up'.[35] Three days later Constable Edgar Budd was killed during an ambush in

Cooga, County Clare as he was returning to his barracks at Kildysart. Homes in the locality were set ablaze in reprisal.[36] At Mullaghafad Cross in County Fermanagh on 29 May, Special Constables Robert Coulter and James Hall were the victims of an ambush, which also claimed the life of an innocent civilian. Finally, on 30 May Constable Walter Perkins, a native of the Isle of Wight and a member of the Auxiliaries for just a few months, was fatally shot when a nine-member police patrol was travelling between Carrickmacross and Castleblaney in County Monaghan. A bread van was commandeered to remove his remains from the scene.[37]

Two days later, on the first day of June, a party of twelve men – members of the Royal Irish Constabulary and Black and Tans – left Killorglin RIC Barracks by bicycle. They cycled across the bridge over the River Laune, past the spot where Constables Caseley and Evans had died just eight months previously, onwards past the high oaks and pines of Kilderry Wood and the three-ring Fort Agnes, where the IRA had ambushed many of them on November Day 1920, and onwards toward the villages of Milltown and Castlemaine.

6

'THE HUT'

Paddy Cahill, Sinn Féin Teachta Dála for Kerry, surveyed all before him.[1] It was a spectacular vista. From his perch overlooking the parish of Keel he had a panoramic view of the calm and picturesque Castlemaine harbour, Dingle Bay, Inch Strand and, across the water, the undulating peaks of the Iveragh Peninsula stretching south-westwards towards Cahersiveen. The Iveragh Peninsula was not unfamiliar terrain to the thirty-year-old. His father, Thady, was a native of Glenbeigh and his mother, Mary, was from Killorglin. On a clear sunny day from Cahill's vantage point, Valentia Island to the south, home to members of the Kerry No.3 Brigade, was visible on the horizon. Cahill sat on the grass beneath the ancient promontory fort at Cathair Con Rí on the spine of the Sliabh Mish mountains, which run down the centre of the Dingle Peninsula. Irish mythology holds that Cathair Con Rí is one of the three oldest structures in Ireland and was named after Cú Roí mac Dáire, King of Munster, a legendary sorcerer and one-time ally of Cú Chulainn, who was said to be local tribal leader during the Iron Age.[2] Two thousand years later, Paddy Cahill was the leader of his own tribe, a group of IRA Volunteers on the run from the British Crown forces and hiding on the remote hills of Corca Dhuibhne, the home of the Gaelic-speaking peoples who occupied the peninsula for centuries.

The morning of 1 June 1921 was 'another of those hot, cloudless days that had characterised the month of May'.[3] Cahill breathed in the Atlantic air. He had stepped out of a camouflaged structure, which had come to be nicknamed 'The Hut', a temporary timber cabin that served as a hideout and as the unofficial headquarters for many of the members of the Kerry No.1 Brigade of the IRA who were trying to evade the authorities and the feared Black and Tans. Most of the IRA members present were from Tralee and had fled the town in the weeks after the Siege of Tralee in November 1920. The selection of the Dingle Peninsula as the base for many of the members of the brigade was no accident. The remote and secluded location in the mountainside townland of Fybough offered IRA members a greater sense of safety compared to their homes in urban areas like Tralee. Parts of west Kerry had become something of a no-go area by 1921, which suited Cahill and his fellow guerrillas. The County Inspector of the RIC recorded that, 'The condition of the Dingle peninsula still remained very bad and the forces of the Crown when entering this area had practically to assume the dimensions and attitude of an invading column. Roads were barricaded against them and ambushes were prepared for any small and unwary party.'[4]

One of those who had fled Tralee and had joined his comrades at The Hut, Billy Mullins identified the distinct advantage offered to the IRA Flying Column by the ruggedness and climate of the peninsula. Unlike the enemy, these men had a superior knowledge of the topography of the area:

We also knew that the British would not dare take on this task as the terrain was most unsuitable to them, the mountain range was high, extensive and dangerous; also it was shrouded in mist for practically five days out of seven; our Column knew every glen, crevice and cliff, therefore British troops would be altogether at our mercy and we would be in a position to take a heavy toll, had they resorted to such a comb out.[5]

A Flying Column of about thirty members had been formed under the leadership of Paddy Cahill with the aim of launching attacks on the military authorities. Members of the Castlegregory Company of the IRA from the northern side of the Dingle Peninsula, under the leadership of the formidable Tadhg Brosnan, had also made The Hut their temporary home. Just a few months earlier, the RIC had led a major round-up of IRA activists in the Castlegregory area so The Hut also offered Brosnan and his men relative safety.[6] The Hut had also come into being because of raids on IRA safe houses. For those on the run, staying at any address for any length of time proved increasingly perilous. The members of the Flying Column frequently stayed at Keel House, a large, early-eighteenth-century dwelling near Boolteens and the home of Mrs Ellen Rae.

Ellen and her husband, William Emperor Rae, ran a successful import–export business at a time when Castlemaine harbour was a busy commercial port. William and Ellen's son Stephen (Steve) was Intelligence Officer for Paddy Cahill's Flying Column and had returned from studying for the priesthood in Scotland to join the IRA.[7] Steve and his wife Greta accommodated many of the IRA men on the run in their small hotel in the village of Boolteens on the main road between Castlemaine and Inch. The hotel was adjacent to the local RIC barracks but despite the danger of using the Raes' hotel and home as a base for the column, it is apparent from some accounts that the police may have occasionally turned a blind eye to the movements of the local rebels. Once, when a Sergeant McCarthy and his colleagues raided the Raes' home for rebels, he allowed one of the IRA men on the run, Milltown's Tom O'Connor, to flee to warn others and he released Michael O'Leary when he claimed to be a caretaker for Mrs Rae.[8] Sergeant McCarthy's decision to release O'Leary betrayed the sympathies of many members of the RIC in Ireland at the time, whether out of empathy with the IRA men and their campaign against British rule or as part of a desire for a quiet and peaceful life as a policeman in rural Ireland.

The Hut – the brainchild of Paddy Cahill and a fellow Tralee IRA member, Billy Myles – was described by Patrick Garvey, one of the men based there:

'The Hut' was a large wooden structure built at the back of a massive rock in the mountainside. It was well camouflaged and safe from enemy surprise. It commanded a view of the Dingle Peninsula and Castlemaine Bay, while to the back it afforded a way of retreat, if necessary, through the wooded areas of Derrymore. The officers of Castlegregory, Dingle, Killorglin and Tralee Battalions were constantly there and had complete control of the western district …[9]

By the beginning of March, work on the construction of the Hut at Fybough was complete and it had become home to over twenty IRA Volunteers. Johnny Connor of the Farmers Bridge company remembered that those at The Hut 'were fed like gamecocks by the people around who were all small farmers and poor'.[10] Potatoes were procured from nearby farms and flour was seized from boats in Castlemaine harbour and taken to The Hut.[11] Food was supplied by local members of Cumann na mBan such as Mary Dowd, Maria O'Shea and Mary Ann Duggan on whose farm some of the men from the Flying Column would make gunpowder for their weapons.[12] The supply of food to men on the run placed additional pressures on the resources of many small farm holdings not to mention the prospect of being discovered as providing assistance to the IRA, but, according to one Kerry Volunteer, 'they bore the inconvenience with great patience and were the unsung heroes of the struggle'.[13] The remote hideaway did not afford the IRA complete safety, however, and its occupants came dangerously close to being discovered in the spring of 1921. Officer Commanding of the 6th Battalion, Tom O'Connor from Milltown, recalled that the police once came within 100 yards of the hut. About this time a letter sent to Major Mackinnon, commander of the Auxiliaries in Tralee, was intercepted by local IRA Volunteers. The letter was secreted within a copy of the *Irish Independent* intended for delivery to Mackinnon. Apparently written by an informer, it gave the exact position of the hideout, the names of the occupants and the number of arms in the column. The letter was anonymous.[14] Shortly afterwards, on 15 April 1921, Mackinnon was shot dead while playing golf in Tralee.

Patrick J. Cahill, or Paddy as he came to be known, was a well-known figure in revolutionary Kerry. With Austin Stack,

he was central to the planning of the landing of arms ahead
of the Easter Rising. He took over the former County Hall
in Tralee and ran a cinema there with some friends but the
premises was burned down by Black and Tans during the Siege
of Tralee in November 1920. As he sat on the slopes of Sliabh
Mish on that sunny first day of June in 1921, Cahill was just
a week into his term as one of seven Sinn Féin TDs who had
been elected in a general election to represent Kerry–Limerick
West in the independent Irish parliament.[15] Politics in Ireland
was in turmoil. Dáil Éireann had been established by the Sinn
Féin MPs elected to Westminster on an abstentionist platform
in December 1918 and an election was held on 24 May 1921
to return members of the Second Dáil. The new Dáil would
not meet until August 1921 and would be sundered by the
division over the Anglo-Irish Treaty, which followed the War
of Independence. But for now, in Kerry and across the country,
Sinn Féin was in the ascendancy and the election results
provided the IRA, through their political representatives, with
a popular mandate. A police report on the situation in Kerry
concluded that after the May election, the IRA 'saw nothing but
victory, and greatly intensified their campaign of terrorism and
violence'.[16] At this time, however, it wasn't national politics but
rather the internal politics of the IRA that was preoccupying
Paddy Cahill.

Cahill had been suspended by General Headquarters as
Officer Commanding of the Kerry No.1 Brigade in April 1921
amid general discontent at headquarters about a perceived
incoherence and lethargy in the IRA organisation in Kerry.
Reports from a GHQ Inspecting Officer had pointed to
battalions working independently of each other, the absence of

proper training and the fact that only 10 per cent of Volunteers could use a rifle. Referring to Cahill's Flying Column, the report noted that it seemed to be devoting its energies to 'eating, sleeping and general amusements'.[17] Sinéad Joy states that Cahill's leadership had little impact on the brigade in the early months of 1921 although it is noted that he appealed to GHQ for arms and ammunition to carry on the fight.[18] Another IRA leader said that Cahill, 'though athletic, was inclined to be delicate. He had pneumonia several times and, though his health was not good at times, he was always hardy and he had great vitality.'[19]

The sweeping changes were initiated at an IRA meeting in Camp in April 1921, which was attended by Liam Lynch, Officer Commanding of the First Southern Division. Lynch's visit to Kerry had been planned for some time and the local battalions were tasked with finding a safe house for a meeting of senior officers. Because Dan Mulvihill was still, in his own words, 'not known to the authorities' (he had only joined the IRA campaign and been active in the locality since the summer of 1920), his home at Brackhill was chosen for the gathering.[20] Mulvihill described the extraordinary lengths taken to protect and disguise Lynch and his colleagues and keep the meeting a secret:

> Liam was the most wanted man in Ireland ... This was the best guarded meeting ever held in Kerry. There were scouts within sight of each other all the way to Tralee, Killarney, Killorglin, and Farranfore ... [Humphrey] 'Free' Murphy was no bother as my clothes would fit him, we were the one height, 6'2". Florrie Donoghue was average

and the suit of a boy we had working for us fitted him. Liam [Lynch] got the pants and coat of a brother of mine. I can still see him holding the pants under his armpits.[21]

During one of the 'most explosive showdowns' between GHQ and local units, Cahill was stood down from his role. However, the senior figures in the brigade remained determinedly recalcitrant in their attitude to Lynch and the army leadership while staying staunchly loyal to Cahill. They refused allegiance to Cahill's replacement, Andy Cooney. As one of those members, Billy Mullins noted, 'all of us known as "Cahill's men" absolutely refused to serve under the new man'.[22] The majority of 'Cahill's men' remained with him at The Hut in Fybough in defiance of headquarters and in their ambition to continue to campaign against the Crown Forces from their mountain retreat.

'Cahill's men' – who played an integral role at Ballymacandy – included IRA members from Castlegregory and Tralee who spent much of the spring and summer of 1921 at The Hut.[23] The IRA members from Tralee included Paddy Paul Fitzgerald from Spa Road, who had been involved in many of the engagements of the conflict and who later took the anti-Treaty side in the Civil War, becoming O/C of the 9th Battalion in 1922; Michael 'Forker' McMahon, who was involved with Fitzgerald in an ambush near Cloghane in 1920 in which two RIC members were killed; Michael O'Leary, who worked in Paddy Cahill's cinema until it was burned down and who was Brigade O/C of Na Fianna Éireann in Tralee; Dan Jeffers, a member of Tralee Urban District Council, described as 'one of the bravest'[24] and Paddy Cahill's 'right hand man',[25] who was Captain of the B Company of the Irish Volunteers in Tralee from 1915;

Donnchadha O'Donoghue, who later played senior football for Kerry; Eugene Hogan, later an undertaker and brother-in-law of the Labour TD Dan Spring; Michael Fleming of Gas Terrace, who had been arrested during the German Plot in 1918; brothers Billy and Jerry Myles from Moyderwell whose sister, Molly was a member of Cumann na mBan; Thomas O'Connor (not to be confused with Tom O'Connor of Milltown) from Castle Street, Tralee, who was a member of Fianna Éireann; 'Big' Dan O'Sullivan, chairman of Tralee Urban District Council and one of the founding members of the Irish Republican Brotherhood in Tralee; Joe Sugrue, who had been involved in incidents including an attack on Abbeydorney RIC Barracks; Jeremiah (Jerry) 'Unkey' O'Connor, a painter from Boherbee, who was described as 'cheerful, witty and brave';[26] and John O'Sullivan of Aughacashla, Castlegregory, a member of the IRB as well as the D Company of the IRA in Tralee. Also there was one of the most prominent and important figures in the Kerry IRA at the time, William (Billy) Mullins from Moyderwell, Tralee. A key player in the revolutionary movement in Kerry from its earliest days, he had been instrumental in mobilising the Volunteers in Tralee ahead of the Easter Rising and was in close contact with Pádraig Pearse before the rebellion.[27] With his comrades, he had left Tralee for the relative safety of the Sliabh Mish mountains in the winter of 1920. From the Hut at Fybough Mullins later wrote in his memoirs, 'we planned and carried out ambushes on the enemy'.[28]

7

'WE RODE ON ... CARRYING OUR REVOLVERS IN OUR HANDS'

In the early morning sunshine of 1 June 1921, 28-year-old District Inspector Michael Francis McCaughey checked his bicycle before he and his colleagues departed their base. The imposing three-storey barracks of the Royal Irish Constabulary in Killorglin at the corner of the Square and Upper Bridge Street was the police headquarters for the district. One of its previous officers had been Thomas Barry who until 1901 was a member of RIC in the town. His son, Tom Barry, who was born in Killorglin in 1897, would go on to become one of the most high-profile IRA leaders in the country and led the Kilmichael Ambush in County Cork in November 1920 in which up to eighteen Auxiliaries were killed, making it the 'most venerated IRA victory in the War of Independence'.[1] By the summer of 1921 McCaughey had been district inspector in Killorglin for just over six months.[2] He grew up at John Street in the village of Crossgar, County Down, about fifteen miles from Belfast.[3] His father, also Michael, was a constable in the local RIC.[4] He had worked as a draper's assistant before first joining the RIC on

15 March 1913.[5] In August 1915, however, McCaughey left the police to join the army and was a lance corporal with the Irish Guards before becoming a second lieutenant with the Royal Irish Rifles during the First World War, serving in India.[6] Rejoining the RIC as a member of the Black and Tans in March 1920, he was appointed to district-inspector rank at Killorglin in December 1920.[7] The IRA's Bertie Scully from Glencar noted that McCaughey was 'a British Officer who was in charge of Tans in Killorglin and the RIC worked with him also. He was a peculiar type.'[8] He was known to take a group of fourteen or fifteen police on night patrols of Killorglin, Milltown and Castlemaine.[9] It was McCaughey who had led his men on patrol to Glencar on the night of 26 February 1921, avoiding an ambush party near the Laune Bridge and proceeding to Lyranes where Joe Taylor of the Glencar IRA met his death.

The party of a dozen policemen under McCaughey's leadership on 1 June was to cycle to Tralee to collect their pay – said to be a total of £100 – from the divisional headquarters before returning to Killorglin.[10] McCaughey, unsure of whether the road to Tralee was passable by motor car or not, figured that bicycles were the only viable means of transportation. By the middle of 1921 cycling had become the main – and safest – mode of transport for the local constabulary as the IRA continued to disrupt police movements around the countryside. Cutting and bombing of roads had become a critical tool in the IRA's arsenal to ensure that the passage of Crossley Tenders and other vehicles used to transport troops was disrupted. Whereas a four-wheeled vehicle could not navigate a trench or craters in a road, bicycles were not similarly hindered: but while a bicycle made for a more reliable means of transport in one respect, it lacked the relative speed and safety which a car or lorry provided. Just a month before events at Ballymacandy, the Kerry county inspector of the RIC had reported to headquarters in Dublin that the IRA 'trenched all roads, blew up bridges, tore up railway lines, felled trees across roads, built up walls across roads, with the intention of making journeys of Crown forces by motors impossible. They have made practically impossible to travel in the dark. Journeys of about 20 miles sometimes take between 4 & 5 hours to accomplish.'[11]

Second in command to McCaughey in the party was Sergeant James Collery (RIC Number 58355), one of just three married men in the group.[12] Since the abandonment of the police barracks in Milltown in October 1920, he had made the daily journey from his home at Main Street, Milltown, to Killorglin to report for duty. Unlike many of his colleagues in Killorglin, who lived in the barracks – there were five resident officers listed there for the 1911 Census, for example – Collery, as a married man, continued to live with his family in a private home.[13] The others who set out that morning from Killorglin were:

John Stratton McCormack (71678), constable, born in Errew in south County Leitrim on 10 April 1901, one of five children of Susan and Robert McCormack, who worked as a land steward.[14] Formerly a rigger and a soldier who 'had seen some war service',[15] McCormack joined the Black and Tans in June 1920 and served in Leitrim, Cavan and Tyrone before being appointed to Kerry on 3 September, based at Killorglin RIC Barracks.

John Quirke[16] (63249), constable, born in County Cork on 16 March 1888.[17] A farmer prior to joining the RIC, he took up his posting with the constabulary in Kerry on 16 October 1907 and was stationed initially at Ahabeg (Lixnaw) and also at Boolteens, Farranfore, Brosna, Duagh, Milltown and eventually, Killorglin. In his diary, Major Leeson Marshall noted that Quirke had spent several years in Milltown and was 'much liked'.[18]

Joseph Cooney (69529), constable, who joined the Royal Irish Constabulary in August 1918. A native of the townland of Annaghbeg in County Roscommon, Cooney was born on 1 May 1896 and is recorded in the 1901 Census of Population as a four-year-old residing with his grandparents, John and Mary Morahan and their son on a farm in the parish of Tumna. He was transferred to Kerry in March 1919. He was based at Glencar before moving to Killorglin. Cooney was one of two RIC members injured during an attack on the RIC at Curraghbeg, Glencar, on 16 July 1920, which forced the constabulary to abandon their barracks. He was also a member of the police party which arrested and killed Joe Taylor in February 1921.[19]

William Harvie (72750) a thirty-five-year-old constable, born in 1886, most likely in Scotland, according to various accounts. Records cannot be found but it is assumed that Harvie joined the Black and Tans some time in 1920.[20] Little else is contained in official records about his background or career.

Henry Frederick John Bowles (70206), constable, born in 1897 in Wellington in the Indian state of Tamil Nadu where his father, Henry Thomas Bowles, was a sergeant with the 4th Hussars cavalry regiment of the British army. Bowles was a plumber before joining the Black and Tans on 30 January 1920 and was appointed to Kerry on 14 February 1920. He was based at Killorglin RIC Barracks from October 1920.

Patrick Bergin (71200), constable, a native of County Carlow where he was born in September 1901, making him the youngest of the group at just nineteen years. Constable Bergin was an ex-soldier and he joined the RIC in April 1920 as a recruit to the Black and Tans. He was appointed to Ballybunion RIC Barracks before being posted to Killorglin.

William J. Twomey (71915),[21] constable, born in London in 1900. He married in 1917. Listed as a 'carman and ex-soldier', he joined the Black and Tans and was appointed to Killorglin RIC Barracks in September 1920.

Frederick J. Beard (71042), constable, born in Aldershot in Hampshire in 1898. Records show that he was appointed to Killorglin on 12 April 1920 following his recruitment to the Black and Tans. Constable Beard had been injured in an ambush at some point in late 1920 or early 1921: in the RIC file on the investigation into the death of the IRA's Joe Taylor, Beard is listed as a witness and it is noted that he was 'since wounded in an ambush and now in hospital in Cork'.[22]

James Hearn (71920), constable, who came to Killorglin as a constable in July 1920. A native of the village of Bideford in County Devon, where he was born in 1895, Hearn was a carpenter and former soldier before he joined the Black and Tans.

Patrick Foley (70111), constable, the only Kerry native among the group and, according to one source, from Inch on the Dingle Peninsula.[23] He was born in October 1894 and had served in the British army.[24] As an ex-soldier, he was recruited to the Black and Tans and transferred from Galway to Kerry in 1920. Foley was, according to many accounts, a much sought-after scalp and it is claimed he was the main target for the IRA at Ballymacandy.[25] Foley, as detailed earlier, had proffered himself as the official press spokesperson for his colleagues in Killorglin following the deaths of constables Caseley and Evans at Hillville on 31 October 1920.[26]

The party of three RIC and nine Black and Tans left Killorglin at about 9.30 a.m., riding in pairs about thirty to forty yards apart.[27] Passing through Milltown about 10 a.m., they arrived in Tralee about 12.30 p.m.

Ten-year-old Thomas 'Totty' O'Sullivan rose early in his native Milltown and prepared hastily for school.[28] The holidays were not far away. A pupil at the Presentation Monastery Boys' School in the village, Totty left his home at Lyre Cottage on Bleach Road to make the short canter to school.[29] Totty saluted his grandmother, Biddy Clúbháin (Clifford). As the cleaner for the RIC in the village, she had earned the nickname 'Biddy the Barracks'. It was a job that ended when the police abandoned the local barracks in October 1920. She was an industrial, formidable woman with huge hands, who claimed relations to the 'Crusher Caseys', the world-champion wrestlers from Sneem. Biddy was speaking with another neighbour,

John Casey. 'The Tans were down the Pound Height early this morning with their swanky bikes and their shiny boots,' said Casey. 'I heard a bit of commotion.' From his home on the Pound Height – the steep hill which descended into Milltown from Killorglin – John Casey had an excellent roadside perch to observe the comings and goings of the village.[30] 'I hear the trains are not running, so they have to go to Tralee for their pay,' he told Biddy. 'Oh,' she replied, 'they'll have sore royal backsides over the Short Mountain this evening, I'd say.'[31]

Totty grabbed a cut of bread from his aunt and ran down Bóthirín Cach Muc (Ordure of the Hog), tripping across the stepping stones of the Abha Solais (River of Light) stream, which had been central to the bleaching of linen in Milltown for centuries. On he ran, past the 'Spout', an essential source of running water for many homes and businesses in Milltown, as well as a local mill and Kilcoleman Abbey.

The Spout was a focal point for the community. There was always a crowd milling around it, and it was a great place to pick up the scraps of news and the gossip of the day while the townspeople filled their buckets for drinking and washing. The talk that morning was of the ongoing guerrilla war, police movements, IRA men on the run and other intrigues. 'Did you hear that the roads were cut back west of Castlemaine and around Listry?' someone asked. 'I heard the IRA lads are cutting up the roads in a figure eight so that donkeys and carts can weave their way around, but you won't get a Crossley Tender through.' Totty turned right at the old Bridewell gaol (then no longer in use) and onto Church Street: a bold child in Milltown would often be threatened with ending up in the 'black hole' in the Bridewell if they didn't behave. The cacophony from the schoolyard reached his ears: there was still time for a game of rounders before Brother Paulinus rang the bell. The pupils scampered up the steps, two at a time to the first floor and the 'big boys' room, and took their seats ahead of morning prayer.

Three miles away in Brackhill, Dan Mulvihill was busy filling cartridges with buckshot with the help of his sister Katie, Michael Scully from Dungeel and brothers Michael and Mossie Casey of nearby Ballinoe.[32] The Caseys, Mulvihill noted, were 'two great willing workers … they were always into everything that went on in our area and their house was a centre which both Kerry I and Kerry II columns, often used as it stood on the border [between the two Brigade areas]'.[33] The Caseys were steeped in republican activism. Their sister, Mary, was in the Firies Company of Cumann na mBan, spending much time 'seeing after the wants of members of the Flying Columns'.[34] By the spring of 1921 the local IRA companies had become 'seriously short of ammunition, especially shot gun ammunition', but Mulvihill had managed to acquire 400 cartridge cases as well as a mould for making buckshot. Paddy Cahill's Flying Column and other units in the locality had also supplemented their arsenal since the attack at Glenbeigh railway station six weeks earlier, through which they had managed to acquire nearly two thousand rounds of ammunition. In the weeks that followed, Mulvihill and his comrades 'made a good share of powder and … started making buckshot' to load some 200 cartridges.[35] On the morning of 1 June Mulvihill had tested one of the cartridges and it 'proved satisfactory'. At about eleven o'clock, Mulvihill heard a shout from the farmyard. A breathless Michael Galvin, a member of the youth organisation

Fianna Éireann and a neighbour of Mulvihill, told him that a cycling party of RIC officers and Black and Tans had passed through Castlemaine on their way from Killorglin to Tralee. Mulvihill knew immediately there was a prospect for an attack.

The RIC, like their counterparts in the IRA, had become adept at modifying their travel arrangements to avoid predictable movements and the inevitable risk of ambush that came with it. The writer Edward Gallagher claimed that the policemen had not made this particular journey to Tralee for approximately two months but evidence from the participants in events suggests otherwise.[36] Dan Mulvihill recalled that just a week before the Ballymacandy Ambush, a party of RIC had travelled from Killorglin to Tralee, through Castlemaine, and an attempt was made to launch an attack:

On the morning of 25th May 1921, Mick Galvin, Company O/C Fianna, arrived and told me that a cycle patrol of Tans had passed through to Tralee from Killorglin. I sent him for J. [James] Cronin, J. [Jack] Flynn, who were in a house nearby, then sent him to collect more of the Company. J. Flynn went to collect Barrett, T. [Timothy] Brick and D. [Denis] Quirke and J. Cronin went ahead to Keel, to get in touch with Tom [O'] Connor, Battalion O.C. Tom sent on word to The Hut as to what we intended doing and asking for help and we would have liked to test the machine gun which we had captured in Glenbeigh. In company with some of the Keel Company we waited at the White Gate [in Keel] for some hours; no one came [from The Hut]; finally word came about 4 p.m. that the Tans had passed onto Killorglin.[37]

The missed opportunity and the failure to get assistance or sanction from The Hut infuriated Jack Flynn and Dan Mulvihill. They told Tom O'Connor that if another such opportunity arose they would strike, with or without authorisation or support from The Hut.[38] The incident convinced local IRA leaders that this pattern of travel by the RIC presented an excellent prospect for an ambush; perhaps the local constabulary were becoming complacent and relaxing their guard. Johnny Connor of the Farmer's Bridge Company later observed that the RIC party travelled from Killorglin through Castlemaine to Tralee 'once or twice a week' and that an opportunity for an attack was within reach.[39] Tom O'Connor and Tadhg Brosnan put out an appeal to other companies for assistance in planning an attack. Johnny Connor was in contact with Tadhg Brosnan and along with Dan Keating and Moss Galvin, he met Brosnan and O'Connor at the end of May to discuss tactics.

Back at Brackhill, Michael Galvin was dispatched by Dan Mulvihill to alert Jack Flynn and James Cronin with the latter making for Keel and The Hut as quickly as he could. Messages were also sent to the members of the local IRA companies in Milltown and Kiltallagh, all of whom lived within a few miles' radius. At The Hut, meanwhile, Cahill told his men that those who wished to go to Castlemaine should do so but why he opted not to go himself remains unclear. James Cronin of the Milltown Company noted that Cahill 'refused to take responsibility' while Tom O'Connor suggested that he 'wasn't well'.[40] But Dan Mulvihill offers a more nuanced analysis, suggesting that since he had been stood down as O/C by Liam Lynch, Cahill 'had no power to release any men'.[41] Whatever his reasons, Cahill remained behind in Keel. Instead he asked Tadhg Brosnan, his second in command, to lead Column members towards Castlemaine.[42] Thirty-year-old Brosnan, a blacksmith, was O/C of the 4th Castlegregory Battalion, 'perhaps the most active battalion in the [Kerry No.1] brigade', and had been active in the Volunteers and the IRA for many years.[43] He developed a reputation as a battle-hardened Volunteer who was described by Kerry TD Fionán Lynch as 'having plenty of brain as well as brawn' and who could 'tear our cell doors off their hinges'.[44] Brosnan's comrade from west Kerry, Gregory Ashe, claimed that the Crown Forces 'had a great set' on the blacksmith and that 'he wouldn't last ten minutes had they got hold of him'.[45] Hundreds of policemen were deployed to restore order in west Kerry in November 1920 but Brosnan and many of his comrades eluded them. With Brosnan at The Hut in June 1921 were his neighbours Michael Duhig, who was known for 'his courage and his calmness under fire',[46] as well as Dan Rohan and Jimmy Daly.[47] Brosnan ordered his men and the members of the Tralee companies who were present to gather their weapons and led them down the mountainside and in the direction of Castlemaine.

At her home at Boolteens, a few miles away, word reached 33-year-old Cumann na mBan member Nellie Foley (née Corcoran) that an ambush was being planned. A loyal and dedicated member of the Keel Company of Cumann na mBan, of which her sister Nora was captain, Nellie had spent several months preparing and sending food to the men at The Hut: 'I cooked for them and paid for it at my own expense and I helped the other members of Cumann na mBan to collect food for them and to raise funds to supply them with groceries, cigarettes etc.'[48] She and Nora had become used to IRA activity in the locality. Battalion meetings at their homes were frequent. Tom O'Connor of Milltown and Bryan O'Brien of Keel regularly stayed there while on the run. Around lunchtime on 1 June, the men from The Hut had been seen running in the direction of Castlemaine. No stranger to bloodshed and providing succour to men who were scarred by battle, Nellie spent the afternoon getting her house 'in readiness to receive the wounded'.[49]

The villages of Milltown and Castlemaine are approximately two miles apart. A section of the road in between is a straight thoroughfare through the townlands of Cloonmore to the south and Ballymacandy and Rathpook to the north. In 1921 the road was bordered on either side by farms and a handful of dwellings. The location did not present the most obvious location for an ambush. Neither flank of the road offered elevation for the assailants to oversee and fire upon their targets. There was no forestry or other natural features of the largely flat landscape to provide cover for attack and, equally importantly, escape for the attackers after the assault. Kilderry Wood, for example, at the other side of Milltown on the Killorglin road was considered an ideal location from which to launch an attack – it had been used in November 1920 for a surprise ambush of police – but perhaps this was the principal reason it was ruled out on this occasion. The IRA men, as Edward Gallagher recounted 'decided to ignore it [Kilderry Wood] because they reckoned it was the obvious spot at which the enemy, on guard against an ambush, would expect to be hit up. Boldly they decided to take up a position which gave them little cover and, on that account, one that the enemy would not expect them to occupy.'[50] In this instance, as in others, the element of surprise was critical.

Ballymacandy was not initially chosen as the launchpad for the attack, however. A small number of IRA members went first to the Tralee road to the north of Castlemaine to look for a good vantage point but found none. Returning to the Milltown road at the other side of the village, they stopped outside Jack Flynn's house, which overlooked the Brackhill Cross junction through which the police patrol would have to travel to get to Killorglin. There they settled quickly on a course of action. They would use the straight stretch of road between Milltown and Castlemaine to launch their attack. It was, as Dan Mulvihill recalled, a good position because 'there was no position.'[51] Men would spread out along either side of the road and lie in wait, but they would need to know when the police were on approach. The all-important scouts who were such an integral part of any IRA ambush came into play: they would be needed to alert the IRA to the arrival of DI McCaughey and his men in Castlemaine and to establish if the police suspected the IRA were lurking in the area. The increased IRA activity would have been noticed by residents in Castlemaine village and there was concern that the police would be tipped off that they were in the area and perhaps alter their plans by returning to Killorglin on a different route. Mulvihill and his comrades knew that McCaughey's men 'would be told we were out.'[52] Earlier that morning, for example, IRA Intelligence Officer, Steve Rae of Boolteens, had been spotted in the village taking a message for Cahill and this would have aroused suspicion among those inclined to speak to the police.[53] It was expected that the patrol would stop in Castlemaine village for a drink. With six pubs there, nobody could be sure where the drinks would be had so Jack Flynn took the guns from a dozen of the assembled scouts and sent two of them to each of the bars to look out for the passing patrol.[54] Back at Ballymacandy, between 2 p.m. and 3 p.m., the IRA men who had arrived from Keel, Kiltallagh, Milltown and the Hut at Fybough began to scatter through the fields and the ditches along the roadside with weapons in hand.

Officer Commanding of the Kiltallagh Company, Alexander 'Sonny' Mason and his neighbour William (Willie) Burke had travelled the few miles from their homes at Lower Ballygamboon through the village of Castlemaine and on to Ballymacandy where they were directed to the roadside by Tom O'Connor, who was leading the planned attack. Mason and Burke were first cousins and lived on adjacent farms opposite St Carthage's Catholic Church at Kiltallagh. Their familial and neighbourly connections no doubt brought them together as two of the founder members of the Kiltallagh Company along with others like Thomas Knightly (Clounalassa), Michael O'Sullivan (Kiltallagh), John O'Brien (Connavoola), James Flynn (Brackhill) and Jeremiah Daly and Timothy Leary of Castlemaine.[55] Another member was Thomas McLoughlin who lived at Aubee, a short distance from the homes of Sonny Mason and Willie Burke. A native of Sligo, McLoughlin had been a soldier in the British army but deserted from his regiment, left the army and became involved in the IRA. He joined the Kiltallagh Company on moving to Aubee and became lieutenant and training officer with the company.[56] As Sonny Mason led his men in the direction of the ambush location, his fourteen-year-old brother, Oliver, was in Killorglin collecting turf at the request of men who were working on their family farm. He made his way on his horse and cart back along the main road towards Milltown and in the direction of his home beyond Castlemaine, oblivious to what was unfolding ahead.

The police completed their business in Tralee by 2. p.m. and set out on the return journey over the mountain and on towards Castlemaine, with McCaughey taking the lead. Stopping in Castlemaine for refreshment, they entered Griffin's public house where they remained for no more than a half hour. Neither McCaughey nor any of his party noticed the two IRA scouts in the corner of the bar. The presence of the scouts likely alerted the publican that something was afoot, but nothing was said to arouse suspicion. Dan Keating of Ballygamboon, who was lying in wait at Ballymacandy, later reflected that the publicans 'were great, no hint in the world of the ambush plan'.[57] While in Castlemaine, however, one of McCaughey's constables, Patrick Foley, 'got a tip to look out on the road home'.[58] Another constable, William Harvie, later gave evidence that, in Castlemaine, the party was approached by Joseph Duckett, the stationmaster at Killorglin railway station, to warn them of possible danger.[59] Duckett is identified in recently published files as one of those suspected by the IRA of passing information to the authorities. He was described as being friendly with DI McCaughey and that he was 'at Castlemaine on that day and told DI McCaughey that they were to be ambushed on road'.[60] It is not recorded how Duckett had become suspicious or aware of an imminent attack but in the network of informing and subterfuge, someone like a railway stationmaster was well placed to pick up on chatter and rumours. Duckett was not unique among stationmasters who were alleged to have been informing the authorities of IRA movements – his counterpart at Cahersiveen, John Greensmith, for example, was allegedly 'notifying police headquarters' about IRA raids on trains in the early months of 1921.[61]

McCaughey suspected that if there was to be an attack, it would most likely take place at Kilderry on the main road between Milltown and Killorglin. He figured they would be 'dead safe' as far as Milltown and could branch off there to take a different route to Killorglin and avoid Kilderry if necessary.[62] At one point consideration was given to returning to Killorglin by walking along the railway line from Castlemaine to the north and west of Milltown, thereby avoiding the main road. Whether bravado or a sense of imperviousness to danger were at the root of his fateful decision, it was one which would have dramatic consequences for McCaughey and his men.

Despite the tip-off and the prospect of attack, he decided to press on and return to Killorglin on the same road they had travelled earlier in the day. The decision to continue while in the possession of this intelligence and against a backdrop of increased ambushing activity in the summer of 1921 makes McCaughey's audacity and carelessness all the more inexplicable. His superiors at Dublin Castle were receiving regular reports from Kerry about the growing number and intensity of ambushes in the county at this time. Just a few weeks earlier, a report from the county inspector to headquarters in Dublin described the growing phenomenon of the surprise attacks on police by the 'murder section of Sinn Féin': 'The general condition of this county is disturbed and unsatisfactory owing to the intense activity of the murder section of Sinn Féin. The IRA loses no opportunity to murder police now. Their attacks are mainly directed against small patrols and individual members. They have at times prepared large ambushes, but for some reason they did not come off.' With an ominous prescience, the county inspector added: 'I think they are waiting for a weak convoy or a bicycle patrol.'[63]

District Inspector McCaughey's bicycle patrol departed Griffin's Bar in Castlemaine about 3.30 p.m., again travelling in six pairs of two. One of the pairs of cyclists included Constable William Harvie and Constable John Stratton McCormack. Harvie later explained what happened before they moved off from Castlemaine: 'Before we proceeded on our way, the District Inspector told us to be very careful. He said that he wouldn't be surprised if something happened before we got into Milltown. We rode on at about the same interval between pairs carrying our revolvers in our hands.'[64]

Half a mile away, sweaty IRA fingers quivered over triggers in the undergrowth of Ballymacandy.

8

'HE WOULD NOT TURN OFF HIS ROAD FOR ANY SHINNER'

Michael Cronin shook the whip and encouraged his horse and cart through Castlemaine under the hot sun and clear blue sky.[1] Cronin was returning from Tralee with a cartload of flour and meal for his father's grocery shop at Church Street in Milltown. The Cronins were one of many shopkeepers in 1921 in Milltown, which despite a general economic slump remained a village with a variety of small retail outlets. The 1911 Census, for example, listed a large number of shops, public houses and other businesses on the main streets of the village.[2] Because of the travel disruption caused by the war, particularly to road and rail transport, merchants were hampered in securing stock so Cronin was one of many shopkeepers who travelled regularly by horse and cart to Tralee to collect supplies. Merchants from Milltown and other parts of mid-Kerry often travelled in convoy to and from Tralee for safety reasons and for fear of robbery. Cronin had left for Tralee early that morning and was returning through Castlemaine at about 3.30 p.m. He noticed a line of bicycles along the wall outside Griffin's Bar and suspected that police were drinking there. He edged his horse forward, turning right at Brackhill Cross and on towards Ballymacandy.

William (Billy) Keane ran across the fields parallel to the Great Southern and Western Railway line between Milltown and Castlemaine. The twenty-year-old from Annagh near Castlemaine was the chief scout of the local branch of Na Fianna Éireann and had the essential information the men in position behind the ditches were waiting for. Scouts had become a mainstay of IRA operations in the war against the British. Ever since the foiled assault on the RIC barracks at Gortatlea in 1918 and subsequent engagements, it was realised that proper scouting and the need for more eyes and ears on the ground was essential, not least in alerting a waiting IRA party that the enemy was approaching.[3] Na Fianna Éireann (or the Irish National Boy Scouts) was the brainchild of IRB leader Bulmer Hobson and Countess Markievicz and had been set up in 1909 as the youth wing of the revolutionary movement. In Kerry, Listowel had an active *sluagh* (branch) from as early as 1911 with the Tralee branch being mentioned in the local press from 1913. Branches followed in Ballybunion, Ballydonoghue, Listowel, Ardfert, Lispole, Annascaul, Castleisland, Killarney, Kenmare and Cahersiveen.[4] Each local *sluagh* hosted social events, lectures and parades and encouraged the 'boys of the Kingdom' to 'awake from your slumbers' and 'come forth with all the determination of big hearts to labour in a good and righteous cause'.[5]

The members of Fianna Éireann on duty on 1 June included Timothy O'Leary, Daniel Moriarty, Michael Casey, Richard

McCarthy, Patrick Sullivan, J. Slattery, Bernard Daly and James Mason (all of Castlemaine) along with Edward McKenna and John Carroll of Milltown. Also present was James Breen of Knockbrack, who was just thirteen years of age, and Edward (Eddie) Hanafin of Ballymacandy, on whose farm some of the IRA men were assembled.[6] Scouts were placed on the Tralee road and on the Firies road near Brackhill as well as on other roads around Milltown.[7] IRA men including John Heffernan, captain of the Callinafercy IRA, who was armed with a shotgun and a revolver, and George Nagle of Ballygamboon were sent to the 'Short Mountain' road between Tralee and Castlemaine in case the travelling party opted not to use the main road and to travel to Castlemaine via Ballyard and Scotia's Glen. They brought with them a stolen wireless radio to communicate with the ambush party at Ballymacandy and had orders to shoot if the police came that way, but at some point in the evening a heavy mist descended and made visibility poor high on the mountainside.[8] The RIC party, Billy Keane told those hunkered down in the ditches, were stopped at the railway bridge in Castlemaine, 'presumably, holding a council of war'.[9] District Inspector McCaughey, in the words of his opponents, had turned a deaf ear to any advice about the dangers of travelling onwards towards Milltown: 'he would not turn off his road for any "Shinner." He would shoot it out with any of them and be damned to 'em.'[10]

An ambush, according to one historian of the phenomenon, 'would seem to be a straightforward matter: await one's target on a known route and attack him when he appears'. At face value, this is precisely what the men hiding on the roadside at

Ballymacandy were doing. But of course the ambush, as W.H. Kautt has explained, was, in reality, quite a complex matter, involving 'intricate planning and preparation, intelligence gathering, reconnaissance, movements and other supporting actions'.[11] Ballymacandy – though not initiated until just hours before McCaughey and his men were spotted on the way to Tralee – had been planned and prepared in the minds of the men present for months, if not years. The weapons had been acquired, the rifles distributed, the gunpowder manufactured and loaded. The intelligence had been gathered: Dan Mulvihill and Tom O'Connor had sent their men to the surrounding parishes with orders for assembly in Castlemaine the moment Michael Galvin alerted him to the opportunity at hand at eleven o'clock that morning. The reconnaissance was in place. Scouts were scattered across the 'Short' Mountain, in the bars of Castlemaine and ahead of the ambush party in Milltown.

By about 2.30 p.m. those preparations were complete and the stage was set. Dozens of men had assembled behind the briars, bushes and trees along the road at Ballymacandy under the command of Battalion O/C Tom O'Connor.[12] The men, O'Connor explained, were 'strung out for four fields' along the few hundred yards. They had assembled between two points: at the Castlemaine end near Clonmore Cottage, a large seven-bay house built in or about the time of the Famine by the MacCarthy's Mór and later owned by the Corcoran family and, at the Milltown end, a cottage occupied by 'Pensioner' Shea, a retired London policeman and his wife.[13]

From the accounts of those present, it appears that every man was armed with some type of weapon. Thomas O'Connor (Tralee) claimed that 'half had rifles, the other half had shotguns'.[14] Paddy Paul Fitzgerald states that twenty or so held rifles 'and the remainder had shotguns'.[15] Tadhg Brosnan and some of Paddy Cahill's men from The Hut were at Clonmore Cottage and each was well armed. Rifles were held by, among others, Jerry Myles, Jerry 'Unkey' O'Connor and Eugene Hogan. The clear instruction from Tom O'Connor, Officer Commanding, to all the members of the brigade was not to move or take any action until all of the targets had entered the ambush zone between Clonmore Cottage and Pensioner Shea's. Only when the last pair of cyclists passed the slight bend on the road near Clonmore Cottage at the Castlemaine side and all of the police were effectively ensnared was the ambush to commence. O'Connor would give the order to open fire. According to Dan Mulvihill one of the main reasons for entrapping all of the targets within the ambush zone was because the range of the shotguns was quite limited and required that targets to be at relatively close range.[16] By 3 p.m. the men were in place, half on the southern side of the road and the other half opposite them. 'Then came the testing time for all fighting men – the waiting time, the waiting for the suspense to cease and the action to start.'[17]

Suddenly, the ambushers heard the clip-clop of a horse on the road. Peering through the ditch, they noticed a civilian travelling on a horse and cart in the direction of Milltown. Michael Cronin was continuing on his journey homewards, completely oblivious to the rebels lurking out of sight. Paddy Paul Fitzgerald, hiding at the Castlemaine end of the ambush zone, spotted him and, from his cover in the ditch, shouted at Cronin and beckoned him to move along. Cronin clearly realised the import of the instruction as he 'lashed up his horse and drove off furiously' in the direction of Milltown.[18] Cronin and his horse might have distracted the already nerve-racked men in the ditches but his arrival on the scene worked to their advantage. The police party on the road behind Cronin had begun to slow down and gather up in a bunch behind the horse and cart. Jimmy Cronin noticed that the RIC had come 'into the [ambush] position in a bunch'.[19] DI McCaughey and Sergeant James Collery, who were cycling side by side, were the first of the group into the danger area. Paddy Paul Fitzgerald noticed the pair slow down behind Cronin's cart and observed that they were 'standing on the pedals of their bikes trying to get a view of the road in front of them over the horse and cart'.[20] Having slowed down, and stopped in some cases, the police had inadvertently placed themselves firmly within the range of their armed assailants.

When the last of the police had passed Tadhg Brosnan's position near Clonmore Cottage, he, Paddy Paul Fitzgerald and those with them, placed their fingers on their triggers. At the opposite end of the ambush zone near Pensioner Shea's, Michael O'Leary, catching sight of McCaughey and Collery, aimed his weapon. Tom O'Connor's yelled instruction punctured the tranquillity of the summer's afternoon: 'Open fire!' The shooting was 'swift' and 'the Tans did not reply to the fire'.[21] 'We fired a couple of rounds,' recalled Johnny Connor, and 'there was no reply'.[22] Under the hail of bullets, which forced many of the police off their bikes, Sergeant Collery had continued to cycle onwards towards Milltown in an attempt to flee. From behind the ditch, Jerry 'Unkey' O'Connor lobbed a grenade onto the road. It exploded and the shrapnel struck

Collery, killing him instantly.[23] McCaughey had fallen lifeless to the ground nearby, having been shot through the chest. The only clue we have as to McCaughey's assailant is the statement from one IRA man who later claimed that Tom O'Connor 'got McCaughey alright'.[24]

James Cronin and Sonny Mason were at the Castlemaine end of the ambush zone and as soon as the last of the cyclists passed their position they came out of hiding onto the road behind the police and opened fire.[25] By this point, all twelve targets were completely surrounded. Cronin explained: 'Tadhg Brosnan was in a position on high ground behind a vacant cottage with two or three more and I called him down. He came down and joined me on the road and just as he reached the road, the firing started. At this time, the Tans and RIC were about 300 yards from us. Tadhg Brosnan and I had rifles and we opened fire up the road from a kneeling position.'[26]

Cronin thought he saw a policeman or two in a field to the north of the road and he and Brosnan gave chase 'but we were crossing the fire of our men and we had to get out'. Michael Casey, who had been with Mulvihill earlier that morning at his home in Brackhill, was 'at the back of the ambush' along with Michael Scully of Dungeel and they were armed with shotguns.[27] When one of the policemen came in their direction, Casey and Scully both fired at him and 'the Tan returned the fire'. At whom the shots were fired and whether those shots were fatal is not recorded.[28] Four casualties now lay dead or dying on the road. Along with McCaughey and Collery, Constable John Quirke lay dead, having succumbed to multiple gunshot wounds, while Constable John McCormack lay bleeding profusely a short distance away.

The accounts contained in the Bureau of Military History provides us with a wealth of testimony for many of the ambushes and engagements during the War of Independence from the perspective of the members of the IRA, Cumann na mBan and Fianna Éireann. This is due in large part to efforts, in subsequent decades, to assemble the narrative from participants in the various attacks in ambushes in the period. Balancing the accounts of the IRA assailants with those of the party under attack – be it RIC, Auxiliaries or Black and Tans – is a challenge because of the dearth of similar testimonies from the members of those organisations. The case of the Ballymacandy Ambush is no different but there are three surviving first-hand accounts from those who escaped the violence. Constable William Harvie was one of the dozen who survived the ambush. According to Harvie, after the group left Castlemaine, and as they arrived on the straight road through Ballymacandy, he heard gunfire from behind a high ditch to his left. He said that the officers dismounted from their bicycles and took cover. Harvie saw District Inspector McCaughey at the head of the party trying to shelter against the ditch on the left:

> I first of all took cover on the right of the road but seeing the shots appeared to be coming from the left, I crossed over, and lay down in the ditch on the left. I was wounded in the head at the first volley and was bleeding profusely. I lay where I was for about 20 minutes. I could see all but one of my comrades lying apparently dead.[29]

Harvie noticed six men coming through the ditch onto the road about eighty yards from where he lay. He managed to fire a shot in their direction, at which they scarpered. He spoke to a wounded (unnamed) colleague lying on the road nearby and they agreed they had 'no choice but to scatter'. Harvie, who sustained facial injuries from shrapnel, made off through the field in the direction of the Killarney road to the east of the village and managed to wave down a pony and trap, which conveyed him to Killorglin.[30]

Back at the rear of the patrol, Constables Henry Bowles and Patrick Foley were fighting a desperate, close-range battle with the guerrillas. 'I saw two men in civilian clothes behind the bank on the other side of the road,' said Bowles.[31] 'Each of them fired point blank at me with rifles.' When their colleague Patrick Bergin arrived, he saw 'Constable Bowles firing at a civilian who was behind a bank on the other side of the road. About 8 yards away on the right of Constable Bowles I saw Constable Foley who was standing in the road. I saw him throw a bomb in the direction of the civilian.' When the grenade exploded, both Bergin and Bowles climbed onto the bank and shot at their attackers, who ran away. Bowles added that he 'had a good view of the two civilians for about 2 minutes when I was wounded in the back'. Bergin said that 'I fired at the two civilians as they ran, with no effect.'

Constable Patrick Bergin was with Constable Joseph Cooney close to the front of the cycling party. Bergin stated that they were jumping off their bicycles when Cooney was hit. 'He fell on his face,' said Bergin, 'and I never saw him move afterwards.' Bergin continued:

I knelt down and opened fire. After firing two shots I was myself wounded in the left leg. I fell on my face. I regained a kneeling position and I saw a man in civilian clothes firing at Constable Cooney. He had a rifle. I had a clear view of his head and shoulders. He was the width of the road from me – about 7 or 8 yards. He was dressed in a rain coat and a cap pulled down on one side of his face. I fired at him with my revolver and he ducked down behind the hedge and I saw him no more. I threw a Mill's [sic] bomb in his direction and then ran down the road towards the rear of the patrol, where I saw some of the patrol putting up a fight.[32]

As the fighting came to a head, the ambushing party suffered its only casualty. Jerry Myles, one of the IRA men from Tralee who had been based at The Hut in Fybough, sustained his injury when, according to the participants, 'the action was to all intents and purposes over'.[33] Running along one of the ditches behind which the attackers were lying was a deep gully. A Black and Tan, accounts claim, rolled into the gully when the party came under fire and he lay there undetected until the heaviest of the firing ceased. He stood up, presumably to take stock of the position, and, looking over the ditch, the first person he saw was Jerry Myles, who was also standing. 'I'll have you, you bastard' cried the Tan as he shot Myles through the shoulder and lung, inflicting an ugly and serious wound.[34] It isn't stated in accounts who shot Myles but we do know it was one of the constables who died in the melee because moments later, the same police shooter is said to have 'panicked' and made his way along a narrow *bóithrín* off the main road. He was spotted by Dan Mulvihill and Bryan O'Brien of Keel who were lying where 'the whitethorn was high and green'.

The pair spotted his 'army pants and RIC tunic' and fired, striking their target.[35] With District Inspector McCaughey, Sergeant Collery and Constable Quirke already dead and Constable McCormack seriously wounded and immobile, the evidence suggests that the constable who was shot – though not killed instantly – was Joseph Cooney. Constable Cooney, it seems likely, met his death at the hands of Dan Mulvihill. In his testimony many years later, Bertie Scully of Glenbeigh (who was not present at Ballymacandy) stated that he loaned the gun of Joe Taylor – who had been fatally wounded near Glencar in February 1921 – to Dan Mulvihill. 'I gave the loan of Joe's gun, a repeating shotgun, to Dan Mulvihill, and it was with this gun, the RIC man, Cooney, was shot.'[36]

According to those who survived the ambush, the whole thing lasted between thirty and forty-five minutes. With the whiff of gunpowder lingering in the warm air, the IRA men began to move from their positions to gather up the spoils of their assault, which would supplement their stock of weapons. Dan Mulvihill coordinated the retrieval of guns and ammunition from the road and recounted that they gathered up 'twelve rifles, twelve bikes, seven or eight Webleys [revolvers], about 800 rounds.303 [cartridges] and 100 rounds.45 ammunition'.[37] Other IRA men searched the bodies of McCaughey and Collery and found on McCaughey 'several dispatches and maps including one of the Dingle Peninsula together with a reference to a proposed large scale round-up of the Peninsula itself'.[38] From Collery's pockets they retrieved between £100 and £150 in notes, 'presumably the pay of the patrol which he had drawn in Tralee'.[39] In Collery's haversack was a document, which referred to the capture of Seán Moylan (Commandant of the Cork No.2 Battalion of the IRA) who had been jailed the previous month.

Most of the IRA men began to scatter in all directions. Some used the abandoned police bicycles to escape, knowing well that police reinforcements would soon be scouring the area for the assailants. But not all of those present were familiar with the surrounding terrain: IRA members from Tralee would not have known how to navigate their way through the fields around Milltown and Castlemaine. Four members of the Flying Column were unable to find their way back to The Hut and ended up getting lost in nearby forestry.[40] Thomas Corcoran, a member of the Keel Company, had been one of the scouts waiting in the pubs in Castlemaine and was sent by Tom O'Connor to locate the missing men. Corcoran 'stepped out of the ranks and went back 1½ miles & found the men & brought them back to our lines'. They had 'got into a wood & didn't know the country'.[41] At Brackhill, Michael Casey and Katie Mulvihill, Dan's sister, cleared up and disposed of the shot and moulds they had been using earlier in the day to make ammunition.[42] Casey was also instructed to stay around and report to Mulvihill any movements of the military.

Sonny Mason led his company back to their homes in Kiltallagh with a warning that none of them was to sleep at home that night. His fourteen-year-old younger brother, Oliver, had been making his way home from an errand in Killorglin and had stopped on the road near Kilderry when he heard shooting in the distance.[43] The teenager was unaware that his older brother was at that time armed and hunkered down beside the road between Milltown and Castlemaine. Realising the danger, Mason directed his horse off the main road into the Godfrey demesne where he waited under the cover of trees until gunfire could no longer be heard. He made his way home to Kiltallagh by another route, avoiding the ambush scene. As he did so, just a short distance to the north, some of the police party who had escaped the ambush, a few of whom were injured and bleeding, were making their way along the railway line between Milltown and Killorglin and onwards towards the safety and respite of their barracks.[44]

As the dramatic events were unfolding, at nearby Callinafercy House, 62-year-old Major Markham Richard Leeson Marshall and his wife Meriel were hosting the Rev. William John King, Rector of Kilcoleman (Milltown) and his wife Kate, for tea.[45] The Leeson Marshalls' guests that evening had first-hand experience of IRA violence. In October 1920 the rectory in Milltown was raided by masked men while Rev. King was at church and a gun was put to his servant's head. But Rev. and Mrs King's experience of the War of Independence was far more personal too.[46] Their daughter Alice Mary was married to the County Inspector of the RIC, Capt. William Herbert King, and she was killed when the couple were fired upon at Mallow railway station on 31 January 1921.[47] As the guests at Callinafercy House enjoyed tea on the evening of 1 June, the major's steward, Charles Stephens ran across the lawn in a fluster. He had heard shooting coming from the direction of Milltown. The major later recorded events of the evening in his diary:

Wednesday, 1 June 1921:

Got to Avenue gate at 5. Canon King & wife came to tea

About 6 Charles said heavy firing Milltown direction about 5. Neither King nor I heard it. About 9 pm man passing by back road said RIC patrol coming home from Tralee to Killorglin had been ambushed between Castlemaine & Milltown. 5 shot, 5 escaped, had come along the railway line to Kilderry crossing then to Cliff & across river by fisherman's boats to Killorglin side.

Horrible ending to so good a day.[48]

9

'BLOOD WAS SLOWLY TRICKLING FROM HIS LEFT EAR'

He first heard 'rapid burst fire, then dropping shots'.[1] William Whinton had been enjoying a book and the afternoon sunshine in the garden of his home, 'The Lodge', at the Square in Milltown when the sound of gunfire reverberated from the direction of Castlemaine.[2] Fifty-three-year-old Whinton had been settling slowly into retirement, having served his final day as a sergeant with the RIC the previous August.[3] The father of eight had spent the final years of his career based at the police barracks in Milltown at the rank of sergeant and he appears to have been relatively popular in the locality.[4] James Cronin of the local IRA company described him as 'a decent type … he wanted no trouble in the district', while Captain John Heffernan described him as a 'fine old fellow'.[5]

The Lodge was the gate lodge to the Godfrey demesne: since his retirement, Whinton had worked for Sir William Cecil Godfrey as a steward and general overseer. Whinton was effectively Godfrey's ear to the ground, keeping him abreast of rumours and possible threats. It was an important role at this time when the gates of Kilcoleman demesne were usually closed, and entry restricted, with access only via a rear avenue. Like others in the village that morning, Whinton had spotted the police party passing through on their way to Tralee, recognising some of his former colleagues including District Inspector Michael McCaughey and his neighbour from the other side of the Square, Sergeant James Collery. Instinctively, on hearing the shots about a mile away, Whinton concluded 'that an ambush had taken place'.[6] He called to his wife, Ellen, telling her he was going to investigate.

Whinton walked quickly out of the village and along the Castlemaine road. Passing the road at Rathpook, which led to Milltown railway station, he continued towards Ballymacandy. One of the first civilians to arrive at the site of the shooting, he described what he saw, in what is one of the very few and most extensive eyewitness statements from the scene:

> On arriving at a point on the Castlemaine Road, about 1 mile from Milltown, I saw the body of a policeman stretched on the southern side of the road beside an iron gate leading into a cottage acre. On approaching the body, I saw another policeman whom I recognised as Sergeant Collery under the hedge on the northern side of the road. He appeared to be dead. His hands were quite warm.
>
> I went next to the first man whom I had seen. His face was unrecognisable. I ascertained afterwards that this man was District Inspector McCaughey. Blood was slowly trickling from his left ear and the jaw was twisted. He was dead and cold. I next saw a constable about 100 [sic] down

the road lying stretched out. He was alive. I recognised him as Constable Cooney. He asked for water. I got him water from a labourer's cottage.

There was another constable lying on the southern side of the road with his back against a fence about 20 yards from Constable Cooney. He was also wounded. I later found this constable's name was McCormack. He had a punctured [sic] wound on the left side of his neck which I bound up with a handkerchief. The front of his service frock was open and his shirt was saturated with blood. He was quite conscious. I gave him water. He said that the District Inspector was the first to fall in response to my question. There was another constable lying further down the road. I ascertained that he was dead. His name I afterwards found to be Quirke.

I then returned to Milltown and caused the Post Mistress to phone the Doctor.[7]

Dr Daniel Sheehan's telephone rang sometime after five o'clock. The medical officer for the Milltown dispensary district was at his home at Glen Ellen a short distance from the village and had seen patients in his surgery earlier in the day. The phone number 'Milltown 3' was well known to the people of the area and Dr Sheehan was used to receiving calls at all hours of the day and night. The call came through from the post office telephone exchange in the village. Dr Sheehan recognised the familiar voice of postmistress, Eileen O'Sullivan. Following a click on the line, Dr Sheehan heard the voice of William Whinton, who was calling from his home in the Square. The doctor was told that 'wounded policemen were lying in the road at Clonmore.'[8] He gathered some medical supplies and his bag and drove in his motor car – one of the very few still functioning in the district at the time – to the Square, where he collected Whinton before proceeding to the scene.

Daniel Thomas Sheehan, known affectionately by many of his patients as Dr Dan, had been in medical practice in Milltown for almost a decade and his family's tradition of tending to the medical needs of the community continues to this day. Nationalist politics was in Daniel Sheehan's blood. His father, Jeremiah Daniel (J.D.) Sheehan, was a national politician of some significance. He fought with the Kerry Company of the Irish Battalion of the Papal Army, answering the call of Pope Pius IX, like many Catholics, to protect the church and defend Vatican City from the armies of King Victor Emmanuel and Garibaldi. He participated in the Fenian rebellion of 1867, after which he was jailed.[9] At the general election of 1885, J.D. Sheehan won a seat for the Irish Parliamentary Party in East Kerry, securing an enormous 99 per cent of the votes cast, reputedly the largest percentage of the vote ever received by any candidate in a British general election. Daniel Sheehan was born in 1883 and studied medicine in Dublin and features in the correspondence of James Joyce who references his appearance on the stage at the Abbey Theatre in 1907 during a debate on the controversial J.M. Synge play, *The Playboy of the Western World*. While at university, Sheehan was an acquaintance of Seán T. Ó Ceallaigh, later president of Ireland, as a fellow member of the Bartholomew Teeling Club.[10] Graduating as a medical doctor, he spent four years in the United States before becoming the resident doctor in Milltown in 1912.

Taking up the role there firstly as a locum to Dr James Hanafin, he fell in love with Hanafin's daughter Irene and they married in 1914. He was, for many years, coroner for west Kerry, attending the scenes of many accidents and tragedies and overseeing inquests in the district. Dr and Mrs Sheehan lived at Main Street before moving to Glen Ellen on the outskirts of the village in 1919. Glen Ellen, located on lands forfeited by Pierce Ferriter during the Civil War in 1641, had been constructed by the Godfrey family of Kilcoleman Abbey for a younger son in the 1830s.[11] The Sheehan's former residence at Main Street was the house later commandeered by the local RIC in 1920.[12] At the outbreak of the War of Independence, Dr Sheehan became the medical officer of the local IRA battalion and as such was regularly called upon to tend to men injured in combat. As he set out for Ballymacandy on the evening of 1 June 1921 he knew, from his short telephone conversation with William Whinton, that it would be those who had been felled in combat by the members of that battalion who were in urgent need of his medical intervention.

Dr Sheehan parked his motorcar on the roadside and, with William Whinton, moved swiftly along the road at Ballymacandy. Bodies lay scattered across a distance of a few hundred metres along the bloodstained road. A handful of IRA men were still at the scene tending to the seriously injured Jerry Myles. He had been removed to a nearby cottage and was laid on an improvised stretcher consisting of two mattresses. Myles' comrades were anxious to get moving, knowing that it would not be long before police in Killorglin and Tralee descended on the locality. Dr Sheehan briefly tended to Myles before the stretcher was raised by a small party, which set off across the fields, flanked by scouts, in the direction of Killorglin and beyond to the relative safety of the foothills of the MacGillycuddy's Reeks. It was past 6 p.m. and by this point, several onlookers had gathered at the scene as news of the ambush spread rapidly in Milltown and Castlemaine. Schoolboys Thomas 'Totty' O'Sullivan and Denis Sugrue. who had heard the shots from their classroom at the Monastery School hours earlier. looked on curiously. Sugrue described the scene:

> At 'Pensioner Shea's' gate … lying side by side were the two leaders of the patrol. A few yards further on the left of the road beyond Denis Murphy's gate was another dead man. Lying against the ditch beside the entrance to Timothy Cronin's, mortally wounded, was a young Black and Tan. We recognised him from the khaki trousers he was wearing under his black tunic. At the end of the line beside Hanafin's gate was another dead man.[13]

As word of the ambush spread, some of the members of the local Cumann na mBan arrived at the scene, among them Annie Cronin from Brackhill, a sister of James Cronin who had just taken part in the ambush and who had fled the scene with his comrades. With the other women, she attended some of the wounded and helped 'to remove Tans who were dying'. Cronin also administered first aid to Jerry Myles and helped to have him 'taken away across the fields about a mile away to a by-road'.[14]

Fr Alexander 'Sandy' O'Sullivan had been on his way to inspect a boat he kept in a barn at the 'Black Gate', as the

Godfrey demesne farmyard was known, when he heard gunfire a short distance away. The Catholic curate of Milltown parish was a former chaplain in the British army and was described as a 'man of fine physique'.[15] A former professor of Greek and science at St Brendan's Seminary in Killarney, he had been appointed curate in Milltown in 1917 when he returned from army service in Greece.[16] He was one of two priests in the parish of Milltown along with Fr Patrick Buckley, who was his superior as parish priest.

Anticipating casualties given the level and duration of the gunfire, Fr Sandy ran to the Church of the Sacred Heart in the village to collect some items and arrived at the ambush site a short time after Dr Sheehan. The smell of shot was still in the air. Fr Sandy stepped between the bodies of five dead or dying men. Constable Joseph Cooney lay in a state of collapse. It appeared as if his left shoulder had been completely blown away and he was bleeding heavily.[17] Cooney was still conscious and the priest knelt to whisper an Act of Contrition: '*Deus meus, ex toto corde paenitet me omnium meorum peccatorum ...*' Cooney coughed and began to mumble. The cleric strained to hear what he was saying. 'Tell the Glencar lads that it wasn't I shot Joe Taylor,' he whispered.[18] Whether the priest understood the reference or the meaning of the comments is not recorded but they were enough to make their way into the folklore surrounding the tragic death of an IRA member in a nearby parish just weeks before. Joe Taylor had been shot dead by police while being marched to Killorglin RIC Barracks. Among the arresting party were Constables James Collery and Joseph Cooney. If IRA accounts are to be believed, Constable Cooney used his dying words to Fr O'Sullivan to deny that he murdered Joe Taylor. Having administered Extreme Unction to all the dead and injured, Fr Sandy returned to the church in Milltown in anticipation of the arrival of their remains.

Forty-year-old Catherine Collery was at her home at the Square in Milltown on the afternoon of 1 June, oblivious to the events unfolding just over a mile away. Her husband, James, had left home early to travel to the barracks in Killorglin to begin his shift. Catherine was nursing her three-year-old baby, Nora, who was seriously ill with tuberculosis. Another daughter, Agnes, had died of whooping cough four days before Christmas in 1915. She was also looking after five-month-old James, who had been born the previous December, not long after his father had taken up his new post in Killorglin. The couple's six other children, Anne, Katherine, Mollie, Rita, Patrick and Thomas ranged in age from one to twelve and those who were at school had just returned home.[19] William Whinton's wife, Ellen, who lived across the Square from the Collerys, arrived: William had heard gunfire and suspected there had been an attack on the police; he had returned breathless from the scene to tell Ellen that there were bodies lying on the road at Ballymacandy; he had phoned for Dr Sheehan and had returned with him to the scene. Mary, Lady Godfrey arrived up from Kilcoleman Abbey: the gunfire had been heard at the 'Big House' and the servants had spoken of a police patrol seen travelling through the village that morning. Together, Catherine Collery, Ellen Whinton and Lady Godfrey walked quickly towards the scene of the ambush.[20] The women knew each other well from organising local sales of work and parish events such as school fêtes and harvest festivals. As they approached the turn of the road at Clonmore, some of the townspeople who had gathered at the scene recognised them. The trio were turned back and warned that it was too dangerous to proceed. In shock and distress, Catherine returned to her home. Other neighbours including Kate King, the rector's wife, had come to comfort her. Mrs King and Mrs Whinton would remain with Catherine Collery throughout the night.

At Ballymacandy, William Whinton helped Dr Sheehan to identify District Inspector McCaughey, Sergeant Collery, Constable Quirke and Constable Cooney, all of whom were now 'lying dead on the roadway'. Constable McCormack was still alive, however, and Dr Sheehan later described his condition:

> He [Constable McCormack] was in a condition of extreme collapse, owing to shock and haemorrhage. He had a wound in his neck which he was able to tell me was an exit wound. I washed and dressed the wound with gauze. I then tried to prop him up to get at his neck. He got into a fainting condition, complained of cold.[21]

The doctor applied a bandage and tied it around McCormack's neck to staunch the bleeding. William Whinton had gone into Pensioner Shea's cottage to acquire a bale of hay to help to prop up the injured policeman, but Dr Sheehan told him that McCormack needed to be moved off the road and to the nearest house. Pensioner Shea arrived with a donkey and cart on which McCormack was placed. On arrival at Shea's cottage,

McCormack was placed on the ground on a bed of straw in the kitchen area and covered with a blanket. Dr Sheehan asked for hot-water bottles and these were sourced from James Stephens who lived a short distance away at Rathpook. Dr Sheehan decided not to further dress the wound 'as I thought it too dangerous, in view of the fact that every time I moved him he got into a fainting condition … [and he] remained very weak'. Whinton had sent a message to Killorglin and told Dr Sheehan that an ambulance would probably be obtained. With this assurance, the doctor left Pensioner Shea's cottage between 8 p.m. and 9 p.m.[22]

That evening the remains of District Inspector McCaughey, Sergeant Collery and constables Cooney and Quirke were removed to the Church of the Sacred Heart in Milltown. As the bodies were loaded into carts, Thomas 'Totty' O'Sullivan and Denis Sugrue looked on. They walked behind the carts towards the village. The barefoot Totty noticed the fine leather boots on one of the slain policemen whose legs were overhanging the back of the cart. The heels of the boots would make a fine cobbled addition to his Sunday shoes and wouldn't they be a memento from the ambush to show his friends, he thought. As he tried to remove a boot, he got a clatter from an old woman in a shawl who had joined the informal cortege: 'Don't you be robbin' and shtaylin' off the dead,' she cried.[23]

Fr Sandy donned his vestments in the sacristy beside the sanctuary and waited at the door of the Sacred Heart Church. It was after seven o'clock and the heat of the day had begun to dissipate. The church, which had been consecrated in 1894, had been built on a site donated by Sir John Fermor Godfrey, partly funded by his sister, Helen, who was a Catholic, and overseen by architect Daniel O'Connell, grandson of The Liberator. On a June evening almost thirty years later, the place of worship for Milltown's Catholics became a temporary mortuary. The bloodied remains were placed in makeshift coffins and laid in front of the altar by soldiers who had arrived from Ballymullen Barracks in Tralee. The coffins remained in the sanctuary overnight. Fr Sandy prayed over the remains and would spend the night in the church with the deceased. In his memoir of Milltown, local historian Pat McKenna recalls the priest's approach when the remains of the deceased arrived:

> When the coffins of the dead were brought into the church in Milltown that evening, they were followed by soldiers with loaded rifles. The priest at the time, who had been himself a chaplain in the First World War, told them to remove themselves and their guns from the church so that he could proceed with the ceremony.[24]

A distraught Catherine Collery and her young children were brought to pay their respects.

William Whinton decided to remain with the wounded Constable McCormack overnight at Pensioner Shea's cottage. At about 10 p.m., McCormack, still conscious, complained 'of a bad pain in the stomach'. Whinton walked to Milltown and asked the postmistress to phone Dr Sheehan at Glen Ellen. Dr Sheehan asked Whinton to send a messenger to whom he gave medication for the injured constable. 'The messenger,' Whinton recounted, 'returned with two tablets with directions how they were to be administered. I returned to the cottage and gave him the tablets as directed.'[25] As he returned to Ballymacandy, Whinton was held up by a party of policemen and soldiers who were at the scene. Whinton impressed upon them the need for an ambulance to take McCormack to hospital. Fr Sandy O'Sullivan came to the cottage after receiving the remains of the other four victims at the church. He waited with McCormack until George Power, Dean of Ardfert and Rector of Killorglin, arrived to tend to his wounded parishioner. Whinton remained in the cottage and kept vigil with McCormack overnight but no ambulance arrived.

Lieutenant Frank Snoxell, a member of the Loyal North Lancashire Regiment who had served in India and France, was on duty at Ballymullen army barracks in Tralee on the evening of 1 June. At about 9 p.m. he was instructed to travel to Milltown and investigate a reported ambush. On arriving at the scene, he was informed by members of the RIC that four deceased police had been removed to the church in Milltown and that an injured constable was in a nearby cottage. Lt Snoxell observed that Constable McCormack had 'a rather dirty medical bandage around his throat, the ends of the bandage hung down over his chest … he was very weak'.[26] RIC District Inspector Hamilton and two Auxiliaries were sent to fetch Dr Sheehan. Having examined McCormack again, Dr Sheehan returned to his home to get a quarter of a gram of morphine and this was administered. Lt Snoxell left Milltown after midnight and travelled to Killorglin to wire an update to divisional headquarters in Tralee. He informed his superiors that four deceased officers were lying in repose at the church in Milltown, one wounded officer was still at a cottage close to the scene of the ambush and that three injured officers, constables Bergin, Harvie and Bowles, were being treated for those injuries at Killorglin RIC Barracks. Lt Snoxell asked that a train be sent from Tralee to collect the remains of the deceased as well as the wounded constable. He returned to the cottage in Ballymacandy the following morning by which time there were a number of Auxiliaries in the vicinity. Inside the cottage, with McCormack, a young girl and an old woman offered what comfort they could to the gravely injured man.

'Large numbers of Crown forces have left for the scene,' reported the *Evening Echo* on 2 June, 'and are scouring the district.'[27] Senior military figures arrived at the scene early on the morning after the ambush, among them District Inspector Hamilton who went to ask Dr Sheehan to again attend to the injured Constable McCormack. Dr Sheehan, surprised that McCormack had not yet been removed to hospital by ambulance, returned to Pensioner Shea's cottage at about 9 a.m. Present was Constable Denis Cahill, a native of County Tipperary who had served with the RIC in Lixnaw and Listowel. Cahill went to Glen Ellen with the doctor to get more drugs for McCormack. By this point, Dr Sheehan observed, the constable was 'very weak, suffering from shock, and complained of pains. His pulse was more rapid.'[28] He placed one eighth of a gram of morphine under McCormack's tongue. Hamilton asked if it would be safe to move McCormack by lorry to Tralee and Sheehan insisted that an ambulance would be required. The train to retrieve the dead and injured left Tralee at 10 a.m. travelling first to

Killorglin to collect the three injured constables Bergin, Harvie and Bowles. The remains of three of the deceased, District Inspector McCaughey and constables Cooney and Quirke were taken from the church to Milltown railway station at Rathpook where they were placed on the train. A photograph published in *The Kerryman* in 1954 shows the coffins being entrained. The train was then ordered to stop a short distance further on its journey at the point closest to Pensioner Shea's cottage and at the rear of Hanafin's farm at Ballymacandy. McCormack was placed on the train on a makeshift stretcher and was carried to the railway line. As the train pulled away, the wounded constable was said to be 'weakening rapidly'.[29]

Major Leeson Marshall went to Killorglin early on the morning of Thursday 2 June. On his way there, he met a group of 'about 50 Auxiliaries and soldiers returning to Tralee'.[30] He met with Head Constable Blake in Killorglin and heard details of the dramatic events of the previous afternoon. Blake – who had come face to face with Dan Mulvihill in his home just a few months previously and avoided assassination – appraised the major of what had occurred, according to the major's diary entry of later that day:

Saw Hd Const Blake & heard details ambush halfway between C [Castlemaine] & M [Milltown], men strung out 400 yds, both sides road. Big burst fire, D.I an ex-soldier & poor Sergt Collerey [sic] RIC so long in Milltown, Quirke & another dead. McCormack (a solder recruited for RIC) dangerously wounded. 7 escaped, 4 of them wounded. In aft M [Meriel] & I went on to Milltown to see poor Mrs

Collery (with 8 children, one dying). Heard more from Whinton (ex-Sergt RIC) living Kilcoleman gate lodge …

Special train from Tralee came 2pm & took bodies & wounded man, roads too bad for motor ambulance so poor man there 21 hours. Dean Power walked over to see him. Gave him lift on way back. An awful shock to us all. God help our country.[31]

10

'GUILTY OF WILFUL MURDER'

On the afternoon of Thursday, 2 June 1921, Dr Abraham Addison Hargrave's phone rang at his surgery in Tralee. He was told that policemen had been killed near Castlemaine and was asked to attend for post-mortems at the military barracks in Ballymullen. Dr Hargrave made his way from his medical practice in the centre of town to the local army headquarters. A prominent figure in the local Church of Ireland, Hargrave lived at 15 Denny Street, Tralee, and was a descendant of the famous Cork-based architect of the same name.[1] During the War of Independence he was Acting Medical Officer for the British army based at Ballymullen barracks and was now being asked to preside over a process familiar to him: the inspection of the injuries of policemen who had died at the hands of the IRA.

Dr Hargrave was no stranger to the bloodied cadavers of the conflict and had seen up close the real consequences of the ongoing war and the impact of the brutal violence on its protagonists. He had, for example, examined the body of Major Mackinnon after he was shot while playing golf in March 1921 and later described how the victim's brain protruded through his broken skull and his body was riddled with gunshot.[2]

The barracks at Ballymullen on the outskirts of Tralee, which dated from the beginning of the nineteenth century, were the headquarters of the East Lancaster Regiment during the War of Independence as well as a small number of soldiers from the Royal Munster Fusiliers Regiment.[3] It was to the hospital mortuary that Dr Hargrave made his way as he entered the hospital building, mentally preparing himself for another macabre manifestation of the Anglo-Irish War. The bodies of District Inspector McCaughey, Sergeant Collery and constables Cooney and Quirke were taken from the train in Tralee and arrived at the military hospital at about 4.30 p.m. Constable McCormack was also brought to the hospital, Hargrave later explained, 'in a collapsed condition.'[4] His injuries were beyond treatment and the loss of blood too great. He was treated late into the night but died at ten minutes past midnight on Friday 3 June. McCormack's death brought to five the number of fatalities at Ballymacandy and meant a dramatic end to a long involvement in policing for the McCormack family – both John Stratton McCormack's uncle and grandfather had been RIC officers. In a remarkable coincidence, it later emerged that as a student at the Presentation Brothers School in Carrick-on-Shannon, County Leitrim, McCormack had been taught by Brother Gonzaga Roche, who later retired to Milltown in the 1950s.[5]

Examining the bodies of the five deceased officers was the first grim task for the military inquiry into the events at Ballmacandy, which opened at Ballymullen Barracks on Friday 3 June. Inquests had been suspended for some time because of the political turbulence and enquiries into such deaths were presided over solely by senior military figures, thereby immediately denying any normal sense of balance and fairness in producing unbiased findings, particularly if evidence was unfavourable of the authorities. For the purposes of the inquiry, the remains of the five men were laid out in a marquee outside the hospital building on the grounds of the barracks complex. Having inspected the remains, the president of the court Major J.L.R. Carey opened the proceedings. Beside him were the other members of the inquiry, Captain C.S. Chambers and Lieutenant M. Wilson, both of the 2nd Battalion of the Loyal Regiment of the British army. The inquiry's purpose was clear, according to the formal report on the proceedings:

> … by order of Colonel Commandant E.H. Willis, C.B., C.M.G, C.M.A., Commanding the Kerry Brigade, for the purpose of enquiring into the circumstances under which the undermentioned members of the Royal Irish Constabulary met their death:

> District Inspector M.F. McCaughey
> Sergeant James Collery (No/58355)
> Constable John Quirke (No/63249)
> Constable J.S. McCormack (No/71678)
> Constable Joseph Cooney (No/69529)[6]

During the preliminaries, Constables Patrick Gilheany and Timothy Moran, both of Killorglin RIC Barracks, gave evidence of identifying the bodies of the deceased men at the military hospital. Head Constable Henry McGill, an experienced RIC officer from County Leitrim, who had been based at Tralee since the beginning of 1921, testified that Sergeant Collery was married and the father of nine children.[7] He said that the other four deceased were single and were stationed at Killorglin. Thirty-five-year-old Constable William Harvie was the first and only survivor of the ambush to testify before the court of inquiry. Harvie confirmed that he and his colleagues left Killorglin at about 9.30 a.m. on the morning of 1 June, arriving in Tralee at 12.30 p.m. The party left Tralee at 2.45 p.m. and rode in pairs about thirty to forty yards apart. He said that they had been warned by District Inspector McCaughey about possible danger between Castlemaine and Killorglin and stated that he had seen McCaughey speaking to the stationmaster from Killorglin. He described the attack and how he had managed to escape across the fields. He 'finally got on the Killarney Road where I met a carter who gave me a lift for about 1½ miles. Then I met a horse and trap, and made the driver take me onto Killorglin.'

The court turned its attention to the medical evidence and the cause of death of the deceased and called Dr A.A. Hargrave to testify. Dr Hargrave told the court that he had examined each of the bodies and made the following notes:

D.I. McCaughey: Gun shot wound on right hand side of chest with large exit wound in back. The lower jaw on the left side was fractured, having sustained a heavy blow.

Sergeant Collery: Wounds probably due to bombs fracturing the left shin and the left thigh, also a gun shot wound in the abdomen.

Constable Quirke: A gun shot wound on the right shoulder with no wound of exit. 2 gun shot wounds on the left side of the chest. A gun shot wound on the left arm. A wound on the right side of the abdomen low down probably caused by the splinter of a bomb. Two gun shot wounds on the right thigh. All the front of the thigh was riddled with shot.

Constable Cooney: A gun shot wound above the collar bone on the right side. This probably injured the main blood vessels. The left shoulder was half blown away as if by a bomb. He had also a gun shot wound on the left arm and a lot of wounds on the left side of the body, probably caused by the same bomb which tore away the left shoulder.

Constable McCormack: A gun shot wound on the left side of the neck and a gun shot wound on the left buttock.

Death, he concluded, was due, in all cases, to shock and haemorrhage following the injuries sustained. He added that he was of the opinion that had Constable McCormack, who did not die instantly, been attended to sooner, 'there might have been a chance of saving his life'.

Dr Hargrave's assertion that Constable McCormack might have survived had he received earlier medical attention was, in effect, an accusation that Dr Daniel Sheehan, as the first medic on the scene could have done more to save McCormack's life. Another witness went even further, however, by suggesting that Dr Sheehan was in some way negligent in his treatment of the dying man. M.H. O'Halloran was the dispenser based at the military hospital at Ballymullen. He gave evidence of leaving Tralee by special train on the morning of 2 June with an escort of military who were to take the bodies then located at the Church of the Sacred Heart back to Tralee. O'Halloran arrived at the cottage at 11.30 a.m. and met William Whinton. He told the inquiry that the wounded officer was then

> … suffering from shock and haemorrhage and in a very weak condition … [he was] lying on a kind of mattress on the earthen floor of the cottage. He was covered with about 3 dirty blankets. I saw no hot water bottles. I asked if there were any. The owners of the cottage were present, an old man and woman. I asked the woman if there were any hot water bottles available or if she could get any. She said that she didn't understand what I meant.

O'Halloran concluded that McCormack was dying. He asked Pensioner Shea for brandy for the wounded constable, believing that 'a stimulant was urgently necessary'. He stated that there was no bandage around the neck at that time, so he applied dressings to the wounds in the neck and back. He telegraphed the O/C at Tralee Military Hospital, asking that Dr Hargrave be ready and waiting for McCormack's arrival at the hospital. Like Dr Hargrave, O'Halloran suggested that the injured man had received insufficient care:

> He did not appear to have been touched at all. His clothes were soaked with blood, and none had been removed. I am of the opinion that this delay in bandaging the wounds would have caused them to become septic and hindered

recovery. I am sure that a man having experience of first aid could easily have bandaged the wound in the back without any damage to the patient.

O'Halloran waited with McCormack until he was placed on the train at Rathpook and confirmed to the inquiry that despite everything possible being done for him at Ballymullen, the constable died in the early hours of 3 June.

Dr Daniel Sheehan was given the opportunity to respond to assertions that there were deficiencies in his treatment of Constable John McCormack. Having been sworn in, he confirmed his movements on the evening of the ambush and his tending to the injured policeman at the cottage. He explained how he had been involved in moving McCormack to the cottage. William Whinton, Dr Sheehan testified, told him he had sent a message to Killorglin 'and that an ambulance would probably be obtained'. The following morning the RIC told him that an ambulance would be secured. Despite these assurances, for a time, Dr Sheehan contemplated taking McCormack to hospital in his own car. He told the inquiry:

> The wounds sustained by Constable McCormack were very serious, judging by his pulse and general condition. Had the roads been passable, I would have brought him into hospital by motor car. It was inadvisable to move the wounded man by a stretcher and bearers to Killorglin. I took no steps to cause a specialist to be brought. I consider that in the condition he then was that nothing further at the moment could be done.

Explaining why he decided not to dress the wound, Dr Sheehan confirmed that the patient was extremely weak and he believed it would be too dangerous to do so. He could not recall how many times he had visited the wounded officer between 9 p.m. on 1 June and 9 a.m. on 2 June but had done so on a number of occasions. He concluded: 'Until the arrival of the District Inspector on the morning of the 2nd June, I was under the impression that the military who had arrived in Milltown that night would have taken him away.'

In his testimony, William Whinton admitted that he had asked the military who arrived at the scene in the hours after the ambush to send for an ambulance for the wounded constable. Later in the testimony, however, Whinton seemed to contradict himself when he claimed that he had not assured Dr Sheehan in that regard: 'I had no means whatever of sending a message asking for medical help. There was no wireless communication nearer than Killorglin. I never told Dr Sheehan that I could arrange to communicate with the military or police forces so that they could send an ambulance or assistance of any kind.' The conflict in evidence over whether Whinton had reassured Dr Sheehan that an ambulance was being secured was left unresolved. Regardless, it is worth noting that, according to the diary of Major Leeson Marshall, the roads were 'too bad' for a motor ambulance.[8] Even if one had been procured, it is unlikely it would ever have reached the scene.

To assist the Court of Inquiry in reaching its conclusions, Dr Hargrave was invited to respond to a short series of written questions designed to clarify his evidence:

1. Does he [Dr Hargrave] consider that in order to stop haemorrhage and lessen danger of septic poisoning, it was of vital importance that all the wounds suffered by the deceased Constable McCormack should have been washed and dressed at the earliest possible moment?
   A: Yes.

2. Does the fact of the said deceased pressing [sic] with a fainting condition if caused to move, justify the abandonment of any attempt to dress wounds, when in order to do so, it is necessary to turn the patient over?
   A: It should have been possible to have dressed these wounds under the circumstances

3. Does he consider that it was of the first importance that the deceased should have been at once removed to hospital.
   A: Yes

4. Did failure to comply with 1 and 3 have any material effect in lessening the deceased's chances of recovery?
   A: Certainly No. 3

Dr Hargrave signed each of his replies with the initials 'AAH'. The evidence completed, the military court adjourned.

In their reports on the Ballymacandy Ambush, published on the morning the inquiry began, several newspapers had noted that Dr Sheehan had done 'everything possible for the seriously wounded'.[9] A week later, the *Kerry People* added that 'after the ambush, it should be stated that the Rev. A. O'Sullivan, C.C., Milltown, all through the evening did everything possible

for the seriously wounded, as did Dr Sheehan, M.O.[10] The
Military Court of Inquiry held very different views however. Its
findings were issued on 20 June, almost three weeks after the
ambush. Captain Chambers proceeded to summarise the cause,
circumstances and location of death of the four officers who
died at the scene as well as the death of Constable McCormack
in the Military Hospital. Among the conclusions were the
circumstances surrounding the death of Sergeant James Collery:

> That the cause of death of the said deceased was shock and
> haemorrhage following the infliction of a gun shot wound
> in the abdomen and due also to wounds probably caused by
> the explosion of a bomb or bombs, which fractured the left
> shin and the left thigh, and that he died shortly after such
> wounds were inflicted, he being on duty when so wounded.

The court concluded the persons who had killed the five police
constables were 'guilty of wilful murder'. In its assessment of Dr
Sheehan's treatment of the injured Constable McCormack, the
court came to the following conclusions:

17. That this Court is not satisfied that Dr Daniel Sheehan
    M.D. of Milltown, Co. Kerry (the 6th witness) took
    adequate and proper steps to treat the wounds
    sustained by the deceased Constable McCormack and
    to ensure proper medical and surgical aid.

18. In connection with this witness (Dr Daniel Sheehan),
    the court finds:

    a) That his evidence is at variance with the
        testimony of other witnesses in several important
        particulars.

b) That he took no steps to inform the police or Military Authorities of the ambush having taken place, and that a very seriously wounded man was urgently in need of removal to hospital although he was provided with motor transport and a wireless station was available at the Police Barracks, Killorglin, within 4 miles of Milltown.

c) That had the deceased, McCormack received proper treatment, and had he been conveyed at once to hospital, it is possible that his life might have been saved.

Finally, the court referred to the fact that the official telephone directory for 1920 did not list any telephone numbers for Milltown nor did it include a listing for Dr Sheehan, despite the fact that he had a telephone at Glen Ellen. But William Whinton had told the court, the judges concluded, that there was a telephone in Milltown post office and at Glen Ellen. Their implication was clear: Dr Daniel Sheehan had not used his telephone to alert the RIC authorities to the constable who lay injured at Ballymacandy.

The Court of Inquiry's findings in respect of how Dr Sheehan treated the wounded Sergeant John McCormack raised the possibility of disciplinary measures being initiated against him by the General Medical Council. In its unequivocal conclusion, the Military Court of Inquiry had effectively accused the doctor of medical negligence and denying adequate medical intervention to a patient in his care despite Dr Sheehan's own protestations and the variances in the evidence of other witnesses. It created a dilemma for the army hierarchy:

were they now obliged to refer the matter to the relevant authorities and, if so, was there enough evidence to have Dr Sheehan struck off? A letter and a series of handwritten notes on the inquiry file, now held in the British National Archives in Kew, give an insight into the considerations of senior military figures about whether to give practical effect to the findings of the inquiry.

In a covering note attached to the file, which was sent to General Headquarters in Dublin and dated 1 July 1921, the Courts Martial Officer for the Kerry Brigade of the army wrote: 'Herewith original proceedings of Court of Inquiry in lieu of Inquest on a District Inspector and 4 members of the Royal Irish Constabulary. The question of taking action against Doctor Daniel O'Sheehan [sic] has been submitted to Headquarters 6th Division for consideration.' Two handwritten notes, with one or two words indecipherable in places, written by two different and unidentified officials, followed: 'Dr. Sheehan appears to have treated this case in an extraordinarily casual way. I think the whole [sic] should be sent to the Medical Association or whatever it's called. It's certainly right to be made public … Do you agree that this amounts to professional misconduct? If so, will you … send on to the [Medical] Council please (1/7).' A typed response from an army colonel is the final note and effectively closed the file on the matter:

No. I do not think the case should be brought before the Medical Council. I quite realise that Dr Sheehan might have acted in a different manner, yet if he (the only Doctor to see the case for 24 hours) was of opinion that it was inadvisable to act other than as he did, there is nothing more to be said. Other people may be of the opinion that a different line of treatment would probably have saved life: there is no proof of this, and to bring a case forward for disciplinary measures, one should be certain and definite as to the facts.

General Headquarters, Ireland, 6th*July, 1921.*

In the absence of any further evidence, it is speculative to attach any motivation to those who presided over the Court of Inquiry other than there being a clear deduction from the evidence that Dr Sheehan had failed in his duty of care to Constable John McCormack. But it is difficult to avoid the conclusion that there was a political undertone to the accusations levelled against him. Though there was no recorded reference to his position as Medical Officer with the Kerry No.1 Brigade of the IRA at the inquiry or on the file, it is hard to avoid the conclusion that the presiding military officers were not aware of Dr Sheehan's political ancestry and his role as Medical Officer with the local IRA and that they attempted – but failed – to blame him for the death of Constable John Stratton McCormack.

11

'THIS AMBUSH OUGHT NOT TO HAVE OCCURRED'

'HEAVY CASUALTIES IN CO. KERRY: OFFICER & THREE RIC DEAD' read the dramatic headline on page five of the *Irish Independent* of Friday, 3 June 1921. The absence of many of the local newspapers from the period – the offices and printing presses of *The Kerryman* and other publications had been burned by the Black and Tans in 1920 – meant that the national newspapers of the time were the first to report on events at Ballymacandy. The report in the *Irish Independent* stated that twelve RIC had been attacked between Milltown and Castlemaine and it listed the dead and the wounded. A dramatic account of the incident followed:

FROM BOTH SIDES OF THE ROAD

The patrol were returning on cycles to Killorglin from Tralee, when fire was opened on them from both sides of the road, at a spot where the fences afforded good cover to the attackers. Before the patrol had time to realise their position, the District Inspector and Sergt. Collery, who were leading, fell.

Then began a fight which, during its half hour's duration, was most intense, the firing being continuous, and revolvers, rifles, and bombs brought into use. After the officer and sergeant were shot the remainder of the patrol sought what little shelter the road offered and returned the fire, using bombs with, they declare, apparent effect. Const Quirke was killed rather early and Const Cooney fatally wounded.

TERRIFIC SHOOTING

The fierce conflict went on until only 3 of the police were left unwounded. Assisting their wounded comrades, they retreated, having left their cycles, but taking all their arms and those of their disabled companions. The people for miles around were in terror, for the noise of the shooting was terrific. When things had subsided, the lonely figure of a woman was seen over the strewn bodies.[1]

'A KERRY AMBUSH' was the *Irish Times* headline on the report from its Killorglin correspondent. After a similar account of the dramatic events, the report added:

The Rev. T. [sic] O'Sullivan, C.C. Milltown, was soon on the scene, and rendered spiritual aid … The dead were brought to the Roman Catholic Church at Milltown and two seriously wounded men to houses in the neighbourhood, whilst three of the others were assisted by their comrades by a circuitous route to Killorglin. All of the wounded have since been conveyed to Tralee.[2]

The incident also made it into the British press. *The Times* of London reported on page ten on 3 June that four police had been killed in an ambush at Clonmore. It added that the patrol was travelling back from Tralee 'where they had attended the Quarter Sessions', though there is no evidence from other sources that any of the officers had attended a sitting of the local court.[3]

By the time the journalists had filed their reports, the only IRA casualty had been taken to a safe house many miles from the scene of the ambush. According the Bertie Scully of Glencar, Jerry Myles was taken on a stretcher across the River Laune at a shallow crossing point at Dungeel in the immediate aftermath of the ambush and 'sent up to us in Glencar'. He was placed on a door, which was used as an improvised stretcher, put on the back of a horse and cart and transported to the home of Jerry Foley, local section commander at Boheeshil, deep in the mountains near the Gap of Bealach Béama between Glencar and Sneem.[4] There he was cared for over the course of a week or so by a Nurse Casey from Valentia, who was based in the locality at the time. Myles was then moved to John Coffey's house near Cloon Lake in Glencar.[5] Members of the Keel Company of Cumann na mBan, including Nora Corcoran and her sister, Nellie Foley, sought out a local nurse, Mary O'Brien from Ardcanaught near Castlemaine, and she was sent to Glencar to tend to Myles.[6] Over the following weeks Myles was taken by boat on trips around Cloon Lake to aid his recuperation but his injuries would impact his health throughout his life.[7]

The remains of Sergeant James Collery were returned from the hospital at Ballymullen Barracks to his home parish on Friday 3 June. His body was accompanied to Milltown by forty RIC members as well as the RIC county inspector. The funeral Mass was celebrated at the Sacred Heart Church at 1 p.m. Fr Sandy O'Sullivan made 'Pulpit references … to the shooting and prayers [were] said for the victims', according to the *Evening Echo*.[8] Collery was interred in the grounds of the thirteenth-century Augustinian Abbey of Killagha. It was noted that those in attendance were of an older age cohort with few young people present, reflective perhaps of the prevailing political climate.[9] Major Leeson Marshall was among those who attended the funeral to the abbey, bringing with him a wreath as well as one from the servants at Callinafercy House. He described the interment as a 'sad spectacle'. Following the burial, the major walked from the abbey with Fr O'Sullivan who told him about administering the Last Rites to the injured and deceased. 'Fine Xtian [Christian] soldier & man of resource', the major noted in his diary, 'Thank God he was there.'[10]

The funeral of Constable John Stratton McCormack took place on Monday 6 June at St James' Church, Killorglin. His death was not reported in the newspapers until the following day. The *Irish Independent* noted that McCormack 'has since died, making the number killed 5. Deceased had seen some war service and had got safely through attacks on a few occasions since joining the RIC.'[11] At his funeral the Killorglin parish priest, Reverend J. Nolan, 'emphatically condemned the shooting and asked prayers for the deceased. Rev. M O'Donoghue, C.C. [curate] also referred to the ambush victims and the shock to their relatives, especially the wife and family of Sergeant Collery, and asked for prayers.'[12]

In the hours after the ambush Cumann na mBan member Annie Cronin, who had tended to the wounded, was one of many who were in anticipation and dread of how the military authorities would respond to the deaths at Ballymacandy. She rushed through the streets of Milltown with a message to 'put away any valuable furniture … as it was expected that the place would be burned that night'.[13] The memory of the reprisals unleashed in Milltown on 1 November 1920 following the ambush at Hillville were still very fresh in the memory and a repeat was widely feared. There were rumours that houses on the Castlemaine road would be burned.[14] Reprisal continued to be a terrifying feature of the conflict. 'As if the innocent people hadn't enough trouble, the British came up with something new in reprisals,' wrote Jeremiah Murphy, an IRA member from east Kerry, in his memoir. 'Where an ambush had taken place, the local creamery or farmers' cooperative store was put to flames. This was in addition to the usual half dozen or so houses which were burned down after an attack. Indiscriminate burning of town and cities,' he wrote, 'under the guise of "official reprisals" was the popular "outdoor sport" of the British authorities in Ireland' as the war went on.[15] The policy was a hugely controversial one and grew out of a shift in policing away from traditional legal methods, which had come to be subverted by the republicans and towards the increased use by police of vigilantism in the place of due process.[16]

In the early months of 1921 reprisals in Kerry were plentiful and often ferocious in their impact. They invariably featured a number of elements: a strong on-the-ground presence of troops for several days after an incident, indiscriminate shooting at individuals and properties and the fire-bombing of homes and businesses, all with the aim of both punishing civilians for the attacks carried out by the IRA and stymieing commercial and agricultural activity. The killing of RIC Divisional Commissioner Philip Armstrong Holmes between Castleisland and Kingwilliamstown (later Ballydesmond) in January, for example, prompted the burning of the local post office and four houses in the locality were destroyed by fire.[17] Also in Castleisland in May, the shooting of a local sergeant saw lorries of troops arriving in the town to burn four houses, a pub and one farmhouse: panic prevailed and the damage ran into 'several thousands.'[18] When Constable George Howlett was murdered as he walked to the RIC barracks in Ballylongford at the end of February, the retaliation saw the village 'almost wiped out' as many buildings were 'reduced to ashes.'[19] In this context, it is apparent why Annie Cronin felt the need to run through the streets of Milltown on the evening of 1 June warning residents of the likelihood of retribution by the Crown forces.

So if part of the police modus operandi in the early months of 1921 was retaliation and reprisal, and given the scale of fatalities at Ballymacandy, why did the district escape vengeance and punishment? Local folklore holds that senior army and police figures were so impressed by the way in which the bodies of those killed had been washed and laid out by local women, that an instruction was issued that Milltown was not to suffer retaliatory measures. It is difficult to believe that hardened RIC and Black-and-Tan leaders were so moved by the treatment of their colleagues by the women of Milltown that they decided against retaliation. There is one reference to a fire at a farmhouse near Milltown in the days after the ambush, which the *Kerry People* called 'A Reprisal', although another report portrays the incident as not being related to the conflict,[20] but there is no evidence of any retaliatory assaults on persons or property in the locality. There was, however, one significant reason why Milltown and Castlemaine were perhaps spared reprisal and the burnings of property that had come to typify the Black and Tans' reign of terror in Ireland.

In the days after the ambush, Major Leeson Marshall received a communication from the local IRA. It was correspondence sent by Tom O'Connor, O/C at Ballymacandy. The major was told that his 'place would be burned to the ground' if there were any retaliatory attacks or reprisals.[21] The IRA warned that 'loyalists in the district' including the residents of Callinafercy House would be targeted. Tom O'Connor claimed the major was alarmed by the warning and 'went into Ballymullen Barracks the following morning' and that as a result, 'nothing happened' by way of retaliation.[22] Major Leeson Marshall's diary does not record a visit to Ballymullen, which would likely have been noted. He did have a visit from an Archdeacon Foley from Tralee on 10 June and he may well have taken a message to Tralee.[23] Whether the major made the journey to Tralee or not, there was no retaliation against the civilian population in the locality for the murder of five policemen.

There may be another related reason for the absence

of reprisals: the officially sanctioned government policy permitting the practice, which was first formally approved at the end of December 1920, was abandoned on 3 June 1921, two days after the ambush at Ballymacandy. But retaliation, had it been planned, would likely have occurred in the twenty-four hours after the ambush.[24] Moreover, it is unlikely that this government decision had filtered down and was known to the rank and file of the police and the Black and Tans in Kerry until days later. Headlined 'Are Reprisals to Stop?', an article in the *Kerry People* on 18 June read: 'Inquiry at Downing Street elicited nothing beyond the fact that the Prime Minister was out of town and that neither corroboration nor denial could be given.'[25] Either way, whether because of decisions at Downing Street or a late-evening visit by the local IRA to Callinafercy House, or a combination of both, the people of Milltown were spared the horrors of another spree of shootings and violence by the incorrigible Black and Tans.

A week after the ambush and fresh from receiving his warning letter from the IRA, Major Leeson Marshall wrote to his daughter, May, who was working as a physiotherapist in Dublin:

Callinafercy June 7th

My dear May

You will probably have seen the news of the awful tragedy that has happened here.

I have not seen a paper since Thursday so do not know for certain, but it is sure to be reported. We went to see Mrs Colleary [sic] next day & I went to the poor Sergts funeral on Sat. Your aunt Mary tried to start off to the scene with her but was stopped by some of the good women of Milltown who went with her themselves. She was splendid.

But the saving feature of the case was the conduct of Fr O'Sullivan. Thank God he was on his way down to K. [Kilcoleman] Farmyard (to look at his boat) when he heard the first burst of firing & ran back to the church for what was wanted & then went to the scene & was in time before two of the poor fellows expired & he got the wounded man McCormick into a cottage & the bodies to the RC church where he stayed with them all night.

He even prayed with McCormick [sic] till [Reverend] King should arrive. King was in Killorglin & came here to tea. We never heard the firing but Charles who was in a field clear of the trees did.

I am thankful I was on the bank & saw all the men there & indeed all Callinafercy working, fishing, farming ¾ hour before it happened so those we are interested in were not in it. M [Meriel, May's stepmother] feels it frightfully, no wonder.

McCormick was in the cottage till 1 or 2 pm next day when a special train came & took the bodies & wounded (3 got back to Killorglin wounded & 4 unwounded) to Tralee. It is said the road was too bad for the motor ambulance. He died next day.

Colleary [sic] & Quirke were in Milltown for years & were much liked.

Mrs C [Collery] has 8 little children. You can imagine how we all feel …

Your loving Dad,

MRLM [Markham Richard Leeson Marshall].[26]

The IRA members who had been involved in the attack at Ballymacandy seem to have been remarkably adept at evading capture or arrest in the days and weeks after the ambush. Few of them will likely have remained at their homes and will have been 'on the run' from the authorities for fear of capture. The only known arrest connected to the ambush came a month later. 'S. Rae, Hotel, Keel, has been arrested,' reported the *Kerry People* of 2 July 1921, offering no other information relating to either the reasons or the charges involved.

The arrest of Stephen (Steve) Rae of Boolteens was directly connected to the events of 1 June. Rae, whose family ran the hotel in Boolteens and whose home at Keel House was used to feed and hide IRA men on the run, had been spotted by local residents in Castlemaine on the morning of the ambush. An Intelligence Officer with the Kerry No.1 Brigade, he was carrying dispatches for Paddy Cahill.[27] Rae had been given possession of the gun used by the injured Jerry Myles in the ambush at Ballymacandy and was arrested in possession of the rifle.[28] Possession of weapons was a most serious offence at the time and conviction carried a penalty of death. Rae was removed to Cork prison. Among his fellow detainees was Eamon 'Ned' Coogan, later Deputy Garda Commissioner and TD for Kilkenny.[29] In his account of events in later years, Tom O'Connor claims that the Black and Tan who had seen Rae in Castlemaine on the morning of 1 June tried to resist giving evidence against him but his superiors warned him that he would get 'no compensation unless you swear'.[30] Tim Horgan adds that Rae's comrades went to great lengths to prevent witnesses giving evidence against him.[31] Steve Rae was sentenced to death by a military court and only avoided being executed when the truce in hostilities was announced on 11 July.

Soon after the Ballymacandy Ambush, the Commander of the First Southern Division of the IRA, Liam Lynch, ordered the abandonment of The Hut on the mountainside in Keel.[32] Fearful of searches and reprisals in the aftermath of the killings, Paddy Cahill instructed his men to disperse. Before doing so, they decided on what to do with the money they had taken from the bodies at Ballymacandy. Michael O'Leary gave £80 to Mrs Rae in Boolteens for the shelter and food she had provided to IRA members in the preceding months. O'Leary used the balance to send himself and six Fianna men to a training camp in Shankhill in Dublin a few months later during the Truce.[33] Some of the Castlegregory men like Tadhg Brosnan returned to their home areas and took refuge in caves and other hideouts in anticipation of a round-up, which never came. Many of Cahill's men followed them, not keen on returning to Tralee despite rumours of negotiations and an end to the hostilities. The hillsides of Keel would be used as a launchpad for rebel activity again: Paddy Cahill and his anti-Treaty IRA comrades would return there in 1922 when they went on the run from the army of the new independent state during Ireland's Civil War.[34]

The five men who died at Ballymacandy accounted for 12 per cent of all police casualties in Ireland in June 1921.[35] The attack was the final IRA ambush of a police patrol to occur in County Kerry before the truce of 11 July. While several British soldiers would die in the weeks after the ambush, on his death in the military hospital in Ballymullen barracks in Tralee in the early hours of 3 June, John Stratton McCormack became the last police officer and Black and Tan to die as a result of the conflict in Kerry.[36] The seven policemen who survived had mixed fortunes. The ambush ended the police career of Constable Henry Bowles. He was discharged from the police on 15 December 1921: his discharge form noted that he had been declared unfit for service owing to 'gun shot wound of muscles of back received on duty' at Ballymacandy. A handwritten note on his file states: 'On 1st June 1921 a police patrol was ambushed at Coolmore [Cloonmore] Co. Kerry, while returning to barracks off a patrol, by a large party of rebels. Five of the patrol were killed and three wounded. Constable Bowles received a bullet wound in the muscle of back and another in the left arm. He has been non-effective ever since.' Bowles was awarded £270 in compensation under the Criminal Injuries (Ireland) Acts.[37] Constable William Harvie, who testified at the inquiry, received a pension of £50 on the disbandment of the RIC. He collected his pension payment from the Collector of Customs in Glasgow, which seems to confirm his Scottish nationality.[38] Harvie's colleague William Twomey also received a pension of £54 and was living in Holborn in London at the end of 1922. Frederick George Beard is recorded as receiving his pension in Derby in the months after the disbandment of the RIC and the Black and Tans. Little is known about Constable John Hearn from Devon and where life took him after his time in Ireland. Finally, Constable Patrick Foley, who had been a key target for the IRA, was shot at as he returned from Milltown to the RIC barracks in Killorglin in November 1921, despite the truce then in effect.[39] It seems that somebody wanted another crack at the officer who IRA man Billy Mullins had referred to as 'a very dangerous character'.[40]

Constable Patrick Bergin meanwhile, was recorded as having 'left the country' soon after the ambush.[41] There is a reference in IRA intelligence files to Bergin being in Tralee in the period after the war ended but he emigrated some time at the end of 1921 or the beginning of 1922.[42] According to police records, he had an address in Toronto, Canada, in 1922 while his wife's address was given as 'Upper Bridge St, Killorglin'. Bergin received an annual pension of £54. He may have had additional reasons for leaving the country, however. New evidence suggests that the Carlow native was an informer for the IRA. Correspondence with IRA headquarters contained in the Michael Collins Papers in the Military Archives notes that 'Const Bergen [sic] was in regular communication with IRA about police movements and activities.'[43] But his sympathies with republican rebels went even further: Tom O'Connor of the Milltown IRA claims that the RIC man supplied him with arms for use against his own colleagues: 'He gave me hand grenades and revolvers every night in the end.'[44] That members of the constabulary were occasionally sympathetic to republicans, particularly as the campaign of terror imposed by the Black and Tans on many communities intensified, was not completely unheard of within the intricate network of relationships between the police and the policed. It was a Kerry constable, Thomas McElligott from Duagh, who instigated the establishment of a police union, who had recognised the 'pressures that nationalistically-minded policemen would undergo' as the revolution intensified.[45] RIC officers and many Black and Tans were Irishmen and despite their role in authority, some were sympathetic towards, if not supportive of the efforts to achieve an independent republic. Neither

Bergin's informing nor supply of arms to the rebels had been sufficient, however, to spare him from attack on 1 June 1921.

The ambush provoked anger and outrage in equal measure within the higher ranks of the police authorities in Kerry. Ambushes were nothing new, nor were the deaths or injuries of members of the RIC, Black and Tans and the Auxiliaries in the ongoing conflict with IRA rebels. Official reports on the incident suggest, however, that the authorities believed the ambush and the deaths it caused could have been avoided. In a report to Dublin Castle in June 1921, the RIC County Inspector referred to the events at Ballymacandy:

> This ambush was arranged in about three hours, by local leaders who in that time were able to muster about 150 men armed with service rifles and shot-guns. The D.I., 1 Sergt, and three men were killed, the remaining 7 men retired retaining their arms. Three of the latter were wounded. This ambush ought not to have occurred, as the patrol got warning of the ambush when within a half a mile of the place of attack. The D.I. evidently thought the place of attack was further along the road. The R.I.C. killed two of their assailants and wounded two more.[46]

While the report clearly overestimated the number of IRA members present at the site of the ambush and contains major inaccuracies about fatalities on the IRA side, of which there were none, the apportioning of blame for the ambush left little room for misinterpretation. It may have been easy to point the finger at a dead man but his dismissal of the warnings he received in Castlemaine about the likelihood of an IRA attack and his failure to find another, safer, way back to their barracks meant that the IRA's success in ambushing his men was the fault and responsibility, according to his superiors in the police, of District Inspector Michael Francis McCaughey.

12

'WHAT DEV DID IN BOLAND'S MILLS, JACK FLYNN DID AT BALLYMACANDY'

On the same day the ambush at Ballymacandy was reported in one local newspaper, new rumours of an end to the War of Independence hostilities featured in the editorial columns. 'MORE PEACE TALK' read the headline on the *Kerry People* editorial on Saturday 4 June, the morning of Sergeant James Collery's funeral Mass and burial in Milltown.[1] Just three weeks after the ambush, Prime Minister David Lloyd George wrote an open letter to the President of the Irish Republic, Éamon de Valera, inviting him to 'discuss the possibility of a settlement'.[2] Peace talk didn't necessarily mean peace however. In the summer of 1921 and in the weeks after the Ballymacandy Ambush, the local IRA was confident and emboldened and, as Tom O'Connor recalled, 'the men were in the best of form and all anxious for fight'.[3] The ranks had expanded and in the Callinafercy Company, for example, which encompassed a relatively small rural area between Milltown and Killorglin, there were 110 members in the summer of 1921.[4] According to Bertie Scully of Glencar, the local IRA companies had been getting into their stride in the weeks after Ballymacandy:

> Kerry No. 1 Brigade was actually tuned up to fight when the Truce came. We had the strongest Bn [Battalion] and our company was the best company. 6 Cos [Companies]: Glenbeigh, Glencar, Killorglin, Milltown, Callinafercy, Caragh Lake, Kilgobnet (toward the Gap [of Dunloe]). We had 9–10 R [rifles] and we were supplied with shotguns. We had plenty of shot. I had 900 rounds …[5]

Talk of truce didn't deter Tom O'Connor, Bertie Scully and others from engaging the enemy. Right up until the official announcement of a ceasefire, and no doubt increasingly emboldened and assertive after Ballymacandy, they pursued plans for further assaults. An audacious bid was made to inflict one final strike on the constabulary. The IRA held twenty pounds of guncotton in a mine near Killorglin: it was earmarked for the local barracks but would have 'levelled that part of town'.[6] The prospects of damage to nearby properties and injury to 'women and children in surrounding houses' were considered, however, and the police and town were spared. The truce was announced days later and came into effect on 11 July. The end to the conflict came just forty days after the events at Ballymacandy and the men who had turned out in the fields between Milltown and Castlemaine that day put their weapons aside, albeit temporarily, in most cases. Jeremiah Murphy from Headford remembered how the Truce was greeted with a combination of relief and apprehension:

The Truce brought about much needed rest for many harassed IRA men and a little relaxation was indulged in. Some who had not been home for a year were able to see their families again, for they had not been operating in their native territory. They were either too well-known, or the districts might have been largely pro-British, or the terrain was very unsuitable for guerrilla warfare. But the majority of the men were able to be at home most of the time and didn't suffer from the worries of the wanted men in the flying columns. Even the British seemed to enjoy the newly found freedom and rode around on their vehicles with little or no arms and less caution. The troops acted friendly but their officers were aloof and sullen. Our leaders cautioned us about undue optimism and warned that hostilities could break out again very easily.[7]

Dan Mulvihill shared his comrade's sense of surprise and anticipation: 'The Truce was on and we could not believe it.'[8]

Five of those who had taken part in the Ballymacandy Ambush would lose their lives during the period of the truce between the War of Independence and the Civil War or during the Civil War conflict itself. The Military Archives offer no clues about how one of them died. Edward (Eddie) Hanafin lived on the family farm at Ballymacandy and, as a member of Fianna Éireann, was scouting the area for the IRA during the ambush. Edward's father, Jack, had been a bootmaker from Brackhill and lived beside Castlemaine railway station. Jack purchased the farm at Ballymacandy, which was bounded by the Milltown–Castlemaine road to the south and the River Maine to the north and bisected by the Great Southern Railway line.

The IRA Brigade Reports published by the Military Archives in recent years make one reference to the young Edward who was just twenty years old at the time. In a handwritten list of those present at the ambush, which was provided to the Department of Defence by Dan Mulvihill, there is one name that stands out: 'Edward Hanafin, Ballymacandy, Dead, June 21.' The cause of Edward's death is not recorded but what is known is that his body was retrieved from the River Maine on 26 June, just over three weeks after the ambush on the road outside his home. The *Cork Examiner* reported the tragic news that Hanafin, identified as a motor chauffeur, 'drowned while bathing in Castlemaine Bay'.[9]

Mossie Casey of Ballinoe was among those who continued to prepare arms and ammunition for a possible resumption of violence. As negotiations on a settlement got underway in London in the summer of 1921, there was no guarantee of a successful outcome. As IRA activist and writer Ernie O'Malley recalled on the announcement of the Truce, 'Would the Truce last a week, or perhaps two weeks? We were willing to keep up the pressure which had been increasing steadily …'[10] The training of the Volunteers and the manufacture of ammunition continued apace. In October 1921 Mossie Casey, along with Dan Mulvihill and others, were preparing explosives in an outhouse belonging to John Browne at Molahiffe near Firies village. The manufacture of homemade explosives was fraught with danger, according to historian Tim Horgan: 'the manufacturing process of what was called "black powder" varied from place to place and the explosives which were locally produced were often unreliable and unstable'.[11] As they made powder, there was an explosion and Mossie Casey was severely burned and injured. He was taken to the infirmary in Tralee and died five days later on 27 October. Another of the ambush participants met his death by his own hand. Former British army soldier Thomas McLoughlin of the Kiltallagh Company continued his involvement in the IRA and took the anti-Treaty side during the Civil War. He was among the Kerry IRA members who took the fight to the Free State army in County Limerick in 1922. The impact on McLoughlin's mental health – no doubt impacted not just by the trauma of the War of Independence and the Civil War but also by his service in the British army during the First World War – was profound. In a house near Kilmallock in County Limerick on 31 July 1922, McLoughlin shot himself in the head but was not killed. The following day, he cut himself with a razor and succumbed to his injuries.[12]

Two of the men who hid in the briars and bushes on 1 June 1921 died at the hands of the Free State forces during the Civil War. John O'Sullivan of Aughacashla, who had joined Paddy Cahill's Flying Column at the end of 1920, remained active on the anti-Treaty side after the signing of the Anglo-Irish Treaty. He holds the unfortunate claim of being the first republican casualty of the Civil War in Kerry.[13] On 2 August 1922 some 450 Free State officers landed on the SS *Lady Wicklow* at Fenit in an audacious attempt to supress republican activity in Kerry, one of the last counties in which the Free State had yet to claim the upper hand. On hearing of the landing, a party of republicans including John O'Sullivan made their way from Tralee towards Fenit. They were following a group led by another of the Ballymacandy participants, Paddy Paul Fitzgerald, O/C of the 9th Battalion of the IRA. As he climbed towards a republican position at Sammy's Rock near

The Spa, O'Sullivan was fatally wounded by Free State troops.[14] Two months later Billy Myles (whose brother Jerry had been seriously injured at Ballymacandy), O/C of Na Fianna Éireann in the Tralee area during the Civil War, was killed. On 20 October 1922 the Free State troops discovered a dugout where Myles and his comrades were hiding near Annagh outside Tralee. While the others escaped, Myles, aged just twenty-one, was mortally wounded.

The only direct casualty of events at Ballymacandy, Billy Myles's brother Jerry continued to suffer pain and ill health as a result of the injuries he sustained in the ambush. In the early 1930s he spent time at Peamount Sanatorium in Dublin as an invalid.[15] He went on to serve in a number of high-profile positions in the GAA in Kerry including as secretary of the County Board and he was also chairman of his club, John Mitchels, as well as being a member of Tralee Urban District Council. Myles' passing in 1950 made national news. The *Irish Press* carried an obituary as well as a large photograph on its front page of some of Myles' comrades from the Ballymacandy Ambush firing a volley of shots over his grave at Rath Cemetery in Tralee. The Old IRA guard of honour was led by Paddy Paul Fitzgerald.[16] The *Cork Examiner* noted that Myles was buried 'within a day of the 29th anniversary of the Castlemaine Ambush … in which he received the wound through the left lung, which left him a semi-invalid and eventually hastened his end'.[17]

Many of those who had led the men and women of the IRA and Cumann na mBan through these turbulent events became public representatives and made the transition from violence to democratic politics. Paddy Cahill had been elected to the Dáil in 1921 and remained there until June 1927. He set up the *Kerry Champion* newspaper in 1928 in which he sometimes wrote about his experience of the Anglo-Irish War. Cahill's lifelong friendship with Austin Stack endured and he was best man at Stack's wedding. Johnny Connor of Farmer's Bridge, who had stayed at The Hut with his comrades, also followed the political path. He remained active in the IRA and was jailed in the 1930s. In 1954 he became the first ever Clann na Poblachta TD for Kerry when he won a seat for the party in Kerry North. He was killed in a road accident in December 1955.[18] Jack Flynn of Brackhill Cross was a prominent figure in the anti-Treaty IRA during the Civil War. He was elected to Kerry County Council in 1926. Like most on the anti-Treaty side, he joined Fianna Fáil that year and won a Dáil seat in 1932. The wartime exploits of politicians during this turbulent time were often relied upon for political purposes and were regularly recounted from the election platforms. A young Patrick Houlihan from Killorglin remembered one such episode on a Fianna Fáil election platform in the 1930s: 'Next speaker was usually a man named Billy Whelan, a wonderful and natural orator with a great turn of phrase. "Republican Ireland is on the move," said Billy, "what Dev did in Boland's Mills and what Tom Barry did in Kilmichael, Jack Flynn did at Ballymacandy."'[19] Jack Flynn was a popular and long-serving deputy but he was controversially expelled from Fianna Fáil in 1943 although he won a Dáil seat as an Independent republican candidate in 1948.[20] Instrumental in his campaign on that occasion was his neighbour, Dan Mulvihill, who encouraged him to stand and campaigned for him: 'My first and last time on a [election] platform,' Mulvihill recalled. Although Mulvihill was a Fianna Fáil supporter and likely a member, his loyalty to Flynn was rooted in the revolution: 'I was not against

F.F. [Fianna Fáil]. I was backing a fellow who had been in the [Flying] Column with me.[21] Flynn resurrected his political career but lost his seat in the Dáil in 1957 to one of his former comrades in the IRA, John Joe Rice from Kenmare, who stood as an abstentionist Sinn Féin candidate.[22] Like many of his contemporaries, as a TD, Jack Flynn spent many hours writing letters of reference for his former comrades when they applied for pension payments for their roles in the revolution.

Fr Alexander 'Sandy' O'Sullivan's encounters with the IRA did not end at Ballymacandy. He remained a high-profile and often controversial cleric with a career including a number of court appearances. Like the vast majority, but not all, of his peers, Fr Sandy was a strong opponent of the 'Irregulars' during the Civil War and a strong supporter of the Free State. While walking near the Godfrey demesne in early September 1922, he was fired upon by anti-Treatyites. The *Freeman's Journal* reported the incident under the dramatic headline 'Priest pursues men who fired at him':

> The Rev. Alexander O'Sullivan, of Milltown, Kerry, was fired at on Saturday evening while proceeding towards Castlemaine. He is a strong supporter of the Irish Government, a big man physically, brave, and experienced to the dangers of war, having served as chaplain in France. He vaulted the wall of Sir [William] Godfrey's demesne, from which four shots had come, and pursued his assailants.[23]

The outcome of the chase is not recorded, but in subsequent years Fr Sandy remained something of a target and an enemy of the IRA. In their eyes, not only had he been a chaplain in the British army, he had tended to the enemy following the Ballymacandy Ambush and held vigil over the victims in the church that night. He was now an opponent of IRA efforts to build the republic they envisaged and which they believed the Treaty had not delivered. In 1924 Fr Sandy received compensation of £20 from the courts for the burning of his boat – which he had been going to attend to when he heard the shots fired at Ballymacandy – in October 1922. The culprits were not identified in court.[24] Even more dramatically, the priest who had heard the dying words of Constable Joseph Cooney – in which Cooney denied being responsible for the death of IRA man, Joe Taylor – came face to face with one of Taylor's comrades in a court case at the beginning of 1924.

Fr Sandy deposed that he had been cycling from Tralee to Milltown when he was stopped by a group of up to a dozen men at the railway bridge in Castlemaine.[25] Among them was Seán 'Bertie' Scully from Glencar, who was described in a Free State army report as 'one of the most active Irregular leaders in the south of Ireland'.[26] The men demanded that the priest stop so that he could be searched and asked if he was carrying dispatches for the Free State army. The priest insisted in court that he was a supporter of the Free State government but that he bore no enmity towards Scully as a result of the incident. Animosity between the pair had been caused, it was admitted, when Fr Sandy accused one of Scully's 'best men' of 'immorality for having brought a young girl to ruin'.[27] Scully's defence counsel insisted that the charges of assault and attempted robbery were politically motivated. Scully was returned for trial, but the matter ended when the charges were withdrawn.[28]

For the civilian population in Milltown and Castlemaine who had been affected by the deaths at Ballymacandy, life in the years afterwards slowly returned to some semblance of normality. But the ambush continued to have repercussions for many at a time of ongoing social, political and economic turbulence. Two weeks after the ambush, in a letter to his daughter, Major Leeson Marshall noted that:

> The country can't be far off bankruptcy as it is, and every week that this depression in trade and commerce goes on is more fatal. Things are bad enough here too, no fairs, markets, trains, posts and universal depression … One does so feel for the people who live in places where these terrible scenes may happen any day and who may have to suffer between the two fires … The difficult thing is to gauge the future. It is hard to say what it may be.[29]

The events of 1 June took a toll on many witnesses too. Most of the injured Black and Tans made their way back to Killorglin along the railway line from Milltown and across the River Laune by boat. Some of them had sustained injuries from shrapnel and bullets. One woman, a Mrs John Murphy of Callinafercy, who saw the injured men pass her home was said to be in a state of 'nervous collapse' a few weeks later. Major Leeson Marshall visited her and found her 'very ill … refusing to eat'. He noted that she 'got a fright seeing wounded RIC passing house on June 1st'.[30] Other traumas experienced by local civilians permeate local folklore.

Having escaped the official sanction or disciplinary action that could have followed the Court of Inquiry into events at Ballymacandy, Dr Daniel Sheehan continued in medical practice. His encounters with the Black and Tans did not end at the Ballymacandy inquiry, however. A few days before the War of Independence came to an end, Dr Sheehan was arrested at his home and taken into custody. Anticipating arrest in the weeks after the ambush, he had been sleeping outdoors in the grounds of his home at Glen Ellen, expecting a visit from the Crown forces. The Black and Tans eventually arrived, ransacked the house, apprehended Dr Sheehan and conveyed him to the military barracks in Tralee. The trauma of her husband's arrest caused his pregnant wife Irene to go into labour and their son, Eamon, later a medical doctor in the village, was born.[31] Coincidentally, Dr Sheehan's arrest and the birth of his son occurred on 8 July, the day on which the formal cessation of hostilities was declared.

Dr Sheehan was detained in Tralee and may have faced a more serious fate but for the Truce, which came just three days later. During the Civil War he continued to treat many of those injured in the conflict. When he was wounded by Free State soldiers during a shoot-out near his home in Rockfield in March 1923, Pat Allman, Dan's brother, required Sheehan's assistance. The doctor extracted two bullets from his leg, without anaesthetic.[32] Dr Sheehan continued to provide medical treatment and advice to the people of Milltown and also served as coroner, attending inquests into the deaths of countless Kerry citizens in a myriad of circumstances until his retirement from that role in 1971. He died the following year, at the age of eighty-nine.[33]

13

'HONESTY IS THE BEST OF POLICY'

After the shooting of her husband by the IRA at Tralee Golf Club in April 1921, the 23-year-old widow of Major John Alistair Mackinnon, Mrs Agnes Beatrice Mackinnon, petitioned Tralee Court for a sum of £25,000 in compensation for her loss. In setting out her claim at the Tralee Quarter Sessions in June 1921 – coincidentally in the same week as the Ballymacandy Ambush – her barrister explained that his client

> had been in receipt from her husband of £200 a year as pin money, and £6 a week to pay her hotel expenses during his absence in Ireland. She did not come to Ireland herself owing to the prevailing conditions. She was a lady who had artistic tastes, and had contemplated at one time appearing in the Cinema, but owing to medical instructions had not prosecuted the idea.[1]

A letter from General H.H. Tudor was produced in court hailing Major Mackinnon's service. The judge decided that if this was a case of a more elderly woman he might be inclined to make a large award but he was of the view that 'this young and attractive lady might take a second husband'. He fixed the amount of compensation to be paid at £9,500, significantly less than had been claimed. Mrs Mackinnon did remarry and in 1931 inherited over £26,000 on the death of her father.[2]

In stark contrast, it would be many years before some of the women who were present at Ballymacandy and their peers were acknowledged or received financial recompense for their role in the revolution. Unlike Agnes Mackinnon, Annie Cronin – who tended to the deceased at Ballymacandy and warned the people of Milltown about potential reprisals – had no barrister to pursue her claim for a military pension for her service with Cumann na mBan when the new state finally came to acknowledge and offer remuneration to those who participated in the revolution. In seeking to meet the criteria for her military service pension, Cronin applied to the Department of Defence for a Service Certificate in 1936. Her involvement in Cumann na mBan hadn't ended with the War of Independence, she wrote. Her activities during the Civil War included treating injured men, keeping arms and catering for a training camp at Kilburn House near Milltown.[3] She was arrested by Free State soldiers from Castlemaine and held in Tralee for ten days. Ahead of an attack on the Free State post in Castlemaine in January 1923, she looked after fifty men. Her brother Jimmy was jailed and went on hunger strike ahead of his release in January 1924.

Unlike Agnes Mackinnon, Annie Cronin had to submit copious amounts of paperwork and fill numerous application forms in support of her claim. Among her nominated referees were the Fianna Fáil TDs and Old IRA veterans, Tom McEllistrim and Timothy 'Chub' O'Connor as well as Denis Quirke, Milltown, Tom O'Connor, Killorglin and fellow members of the A Company of Cumann na mBan. Cronin's Civil War involvement was not initially accepted as part of her claim and on appeal, like other applicants going through the process, she was required to give evidence to an investigating officer in 1942. She was eventually awarded a payment for over two years' service. In December 1967 she received two pension cheques in the post by mistake, effectively a double payment caused by an apparent clerical error. Cronin sent one of the cheques back with a covering note:

> Brackhill, Castlemaine, Dec. 29th, 1967
>
> A chara,
>
> Received two cheques this morning. I am returning one as 'Honesty is the best of Policy.' It was a mistake as any person is liable to forget these times. Wishing you all in the Dept a very Happy and Prosperous New Year.
>
> From Annie J. Cronin.

Cronin was also awarded a pension of £77 per annum in 1965. Again, supporting documentation was required and Dr Eamon 'Bunny' Sheehan, son of Dr Daniel Sheehan, submitted a medical report to the department, which concluded that she was unfit for work because of physical ailments including arthritis. An itemised list of the amount of milk supplied by her brother, John, to Castlemaine Creamery for the previous year was also required to fully assess her means. The pension payment was reduced, however, when Cronin became eligible for the statutory old-age pension in 1971. She wrote to Timothy 'Chub' O'Connor TD wondering 'if that's the treatment I deserve in my old age'. Her ailing brother John and herself 'never gave this [Fianna Fáil] Government a bad turn, always backed them'. On the sale of the Cronin family farm at Brackhill in 1973, the Special Allowance she had been awarded in 1943 was terminated by the department. In later years, Cronin was a resident at St Joseph's Nursing Home in Killorglin and Carrigoran House, Newmarket on Fergus, in Clare. She died on 30 July 1984. Her solicitor confirmed her passing to the department and noted that 'the deceased had very little assets as of the date of her death'.[4]

Cronin's is one of the many thousands of applications for payments, allowances and pensions, which were submitted to the Department of Defence in the years after the revolution under the provisions of various Army Pensions Acts and the Military Service Pensions Acts between 1922 and 1953, and which are held in the Military Archives at Cathal Brugha Barracks in Dublin. Applicants were assessed by the Department of Defence through a board of assessors and an advisory committee established under the relevant legislation, and were deemed eligible or not.[5] The process required the filling of an application form itemising one's role in the revolution and accompanying testimonies for referees, usually senior figures in, for example, the IRA, who would vouch for an applicant's claim.

Among those appointed to the Advisory Committee in 1950 was Dan Mulvihill who travelled around the country to hear testimonies from applicants. He was also a member of the Board of Assessors, which was required to examine every application for a certificate of military service referred to it by the Minister for Defence and consider the eligibility of applicants.[6] Mulvihill adopted a sympathetic approach of trying to help applicants who were 'down and out'.[7] The bar was set high, however, for those seeking remuneration: the pension files are replete with appeals from Volunteers turned down for payments of allowances and pensions, and the majority of applications were rejected. According to a report in 1957, for example, of the 82,000 applications made under Acts of 1924 and 1934, just 15,700 or just one fifth were successful. This left 'a significant constituency of dissatisfaction among veterans refused pensions'.[8] Whether from successful pension applicants or not, the accounts – often accompanied by handwritten details of ambushes, killings, gun-running and other incidents – offer 'a window into every parish and townland in this country and the activities undertaken by ordinary people pursuing the ambition of nationhood'.[9] The pension applications complement the witness statements held by the Bureau of Military History, which include first-hand accounts from almost 1,800 participants and other material collected in the 1940s and 1950s through a state-sponsored exercise to gather the accounts of those involved in the revolution between 1913 and 1921.

Annie Cronin was just one of many of the protagonists at Ballymacandy who applied for payments in the decades after Independence and whose stories are emerging now for the first time. Dan Mulvihill's sister Katie, who was helping to make gunpowder on the morning of the ambush, was 'regularly under fire' as she carried guns and ammunition and continued to shelter men during the Civil War was not awarded a pension until 1961 following lengthy correspondence about her claim. At the time of her death, aged eighty-nine at the County Home in Killarney in 1981, she was in receipt of a monthly pension of £17.20.[10] 'My sister … died yesterday,' wrote her brother in a letter to the department, 'let me know what the procedure is. Do you require a death Cert. I am the only one of family left alive.'[11] Amelia Mason, meanwhile, whose home at Brackhill (where she lived with her husband, Sonny Mason of the Kiltallagh IRA) had been repeatedly raided for arms, spent many years trying to secure recompense. Illness prevented her from attending for interview with the Board of Assessors and there followed much toing and froing to secure a positive outcome. Her initial application for a pension was rejected but following a successful appeal, Mason was awarded a pension of £9 6s. 1d. in 1944 for just short of two years of active service, thanks in part to a letter from Tom McEllistrim TD who described her service in the period as 'outstanding'.

It wasn't just members of Cumann na mBan who had difficulty proving their involvement in incidents in this period. A scout on duty on 1 June 1921, James Breen of Knockbrack, Firies, was a thirteen-year-old member of Fianna Éireann when he gathered up some of the weapons strewn on the road as the bodies were removed from the scene at Ballymacandy. In later years Breen applied for a military pension as well as a service medal. He initially claimed membership of the IRA on the basis that each local Fianna *sluagh* (branch) operated under the direction of the nearest IRA company. He required correspondence from Michael O'Leary, who was O/C of the Fianna with the Kerry No.1 Brigade to verify his membership and to explain that the *sluagh* operated under the control of the local IRA company. He was also required to prove his date of birth amid confusion about his age and a suspicion that he must have been too young to have been involved in the ambush. Deputy Tom McEllistrim vouched for Breen's involvement in the organisation and he eventually received his medal in the 1950s and a pension in the 1960s.[12]

The vagaries of the pensions process and the challenges facing applicants is also highlighted by the different approaches to the applications of the Corcoran sisters of Boolteens, Keel, whose pension applications generated significantly different responses from the Department of Defence despite very similar applications. Nora Corcoran and her sister, Nellie Foley, had remarkably similar service records according to their own accounts and those of their referees. As detailed in Chapter Two, their home was a safehouse for IRA members on the run; men were treated and cared for in their front room; and they were both engaged in first-aid work, carrying dispatches, preparing food for the men at The Hut and storing arms near their home. IRA battalion meetings were hosted in their house. All that distinguishes them from an analysis of their pension applications is the role played by Nora as Keel Company Captain while Nellie had no stated rank within the organisation. Their work with Cumann na mBan did not end with the War of Independence. Their bespoke 'dressing station' continued to host wounded men 'when nobody else would' during the Civil War.

Among those they looked after was Tom O'Connor, who stated that he had been nursed by the sisters after he was shot through the lung and arm in County Limerick in July 1922.[13] They dressed wounds and procured the services of doctors and nurses 'at great risk and inconvenience' and found alternative accommodation for the injured when they were tipped off about a possible raid by the Free State forces, which happened several times.[14] Soldiers fired a shot outside their home, threatened to kill one of their farm workers and took away their horse.[15]

While the accounts provided by Nora and Nellie, as well as the testimonies and references of local IRA leaders, are remarkably similar – and almost verbatim in many respects – the decisions on their applications were quite different. Nora received an annual pension payment of £18 15s. in 1942 relating to almost four years of service but Nellie's claim was successful only in respect of two and a half years.[16] Nellie's claim had been initially rejected by the Board of Assessors but she was granted, on appeal, a pension payment of £14 3s. A note on Nellie's file written by a department official suggests, however, that the Department of Defence believed the older sister, Nora, who was company captain, was the more significant and important participant in events:

> This lady [Nellie] and her sister [Nora] who were spinsters at the time appear to have been doing a good deal of work for the IRA. Her sister [Nora] was the Capt. of the Cumann na mBan and, so far as I can gather, the present applicant [Nellie] played the part of Martha. Her job was to look after the home and she did not really become active until 1920.[17]

The biblical reference to the Gospel according to Luke and the story of Jesus' visit to the home of Martha and Mary means that the department had decided that Nora, like Mary – who sat at Jesus' feet while he preached – was the more deserving recipient, while her sister Nellie, like Martha, who prepared food for Jesus, was a less worthy applicant.[18] That two sisters living in the same home and essentially involved in the same activities at the same time had such different experiences with the Department of Defence shows how challenging it was for many participants to secure recompense. Nellie Foley had a short time in which to enjoy her pension – she was awarded her pension in 1942 and died in 1949. Nora, who was a teacher for many years at Castledrum National School, died in 1958.

The pension files also shine a light on examples of financial hardship and emigration experienced by many of those who took part in the campaign for independence as well as participants at Ballymacandy. As Diarmaid Ferriter has suggested, the level of dependency on the pensions as a source of income for many veterans and their survivors 'permeates the Military Service pension files.'[19] Dan Mulvihill and his family fell on hard times after the foundation of the Irish State. The family sold their farm in 1924 and moved to another house nearby. Tom O'Connor, O/C at Ballymacandy, lodged a claim for a pension payment with the Department of Defence in 1933. O'Connor had been shot through the lung in 1922, rendering his left arm and hand 'practically useless'. The injury put paid to his work as a farmer and O'Connor was forced to emigrate to Canada and the United States. He applied for several jobs there 'but was always turned down by the Doctor's on account of my hand.'[20] O'Connor married Delia Courtney, a former member of Cumann na mBan, and returned to live in Killorglin in 1931

where he ran a shop until the mid-1960s.[21] He was awarded
five-years' service for pension purposes in 1935.

In other cases applicants did not seek recompense until
absolutely necessary. Mary Riordan (*née* Casey) from Ballinoe,
whose brother Mossie Casey joined the fight at Ballymacandy
and died in an accident while making explosives in October
1921, only applied for a payment in 1951: 'This is my first
application for a service pension as I didn't think I needed it but
now circumstances compel me to seek some consideration and
compensation for my services while attached to the Cumann
na mBan.'[22] Mary and Mossie's father, Maurice Casey, applied
for compensation under the Army Pensions Acts following the
death of his son and insisted he had to hire a labourer to assist
with the farm work, which Mossie had done until he was killed.
The Department of Defence found, however, that Maurice Snr
was not dependent on the deceased for financial support.[23]
Garda Edward Nagle of Milltown Garda Station claimed that
Casey was 'a very independent farmer. He still works on his
farm and never was dependent on his son.'[24] Meanwhile,
Thomas Corcoran – who scouted in a bar in Castlemaine on
the day of the Ballymacandy Ambush – felt that this relatively
minor role was held against him by the assessors. On appealing
a decision to deny him a pension, Corcoran asked how he
could have partaken in the fighting if he was simply obeying
an order of a superior officer:

> I went to the place of ambush with some of my company
> and took my place inside the fence with my shot gun
> fully intended to fight, until the two O/Cs Dan Mulvihill
> and Bernard [Bryan] O'Brien came up and sent me to

Castlemaine village to look after more pressing & urgent business there. Well then I couldn't be in the shooting unless I disobeyed orders although I knew my job was more dangerous than to stay inside the fence.[25]

Corcoran's appeal was upheld and he was in receipt of an annual payment of £23.76 at the time of his death in 1971.

The emigration that ravaged Ireland for decades after the foundation of the Free State is a recurrent theme which surfaces in the pension files. It has been pointed out that reasons for emigration were manifold and primarily related to the prevailing economic situation and a lack of employment opportunities.[26] However, among the records of Cumann na mBan members, it was noted that a 'good number' of the fifty members of the Keel Company had left for Australia, New Zealand and the US by the late 1930s.[27] Tadhg Brosnan, Michael Duhig and Dan Rohan of Castlegregory, who had stayed at the Hut at Fybough and were present for the ambush at Ballymacandy, were among those who went to America. In his book *Fighting for the Cause*, Tim Horgan describes Brosnan's journey from Ireland to Ellis Island in 1924 and from there to becoming a central figure in Irish republicanism in the United States as a member of the Kerrymen's Irish Republican Club and the influential Clan na Gael.[28] Such was his status in Irish-American circles that he was approached to stand for election for Fianna Fáil after the party's foundation in his native country in 1926 but he declined.[29] In later years Brosnan and Duhig became involved in Noraid, which was linked to raising money in the US for the Provisional IRA. Brosnan died in New York in 1971, Duhig in Chicago in 1980.[30] The fact that many veterans of the period were abroad presented its own challenges in terms of the payment of pensions and allowances. Edward Langford of the Callinafercy Company, for example, spent many years in the United States at up to eight different addresses and had occasion to write to the Department of Defence in the 1950s to check the whereabouts of his most recent payment.[31] Langford was just one of many republican fighters 'who ultimately could not afford to remain in the country they fought to free'.[32]

Major Leeson Marshall, whose diaries and letters provide a remarkable insight into the everyday events of this period, continued to live on at Callinafercy until his death in 1939.[33] Despite his home being raided for guns and supplies on four different occasions, the major's political acumen and the esteem in which he was held by his own neighbours saved the house. His diaries make it clear that he was not a character isolated from his community as over and over, there are entries mentioning local funerals he attended, farmers assisted and money and support distributed to the needy. Although intensely loyal to the Crown and the typification of an Anglo-Irish gentleman, Callinafercy was his home and his emotional soundboard. His diaries also show that life after the Civil War returned to its old form remarkably quickly. His daughter's wedding reception in July 1924 was held at Callinafercy and was a significant society event in Milltown; he employed former IRA volunteers to patrol the grounds on the day of the wedding to prevent trespass, noting in his diary how smart the men looked in their blue uniforms.

In his later years the major suffered declining health: his eyesight deteriorated greatly and his letters became almost illegible. Having been through the First World War, the threat of another war looming was incomprehensible to him. He died on 13 December 1939, a few weeks short of his eightieth birthday. Among the masses of sympathy letters was one written by Liam Burke, private secretary to Liam Cosgrave, expressing sympathy on behalf of Cosgrave and the Fine Gael Standing Committee.[34] More personally, Hannah Sugrue, a servant at Kilcoleman when the ambush of Ballymacandy took place, wrote to his daughter, 'Callinafercy and the surrounding districts has lost a good friend who was always ready to help them out in all their troubles.'[35]

IRA members and their families were not the only ones to suffer personally and financially after the revolution ended. The speedy and substantial compensation awarded to Agnes Beatrice Mackinnon in the aftermath of her husband's assassination contrasted not only with the relative paucity of payments and complexity of the application process for pensions and allowances for members of the IRA and Cumann na mBan; it also often stands in contrast to the financial recompense provided to the widows and dependants of the lowers ranks of the police.

Police historian Donal O'Sullivan claims that 'the hardship endured by widows and children following the deaths of members was extreme.'[36] James Collery's death at Ballymacandy deprived his wife Catherine of a husband and his eight surviving children of a father, and with his passing went his salary, which was the household's only source of income. The family left Milltown in the weeks after the ambush and lived for a short time in Tralee before moving to Limerick city in

November where Catherine's brother helped to purchase a house to accommodate the young family. Having lost her fifth-born, Agnes, to whooping cough in 1915, three-year-old Nora died on 4 October 1921, just four months after her father was killed. The cause of Nora's death was '*tabes mesenterica*' – the obscure term for a debilitating tubercular infection of the lymph glands.[37]

According to records held by the Bureau of Military History and police records in the British Archives, Mrs Collery and her children received a compensation award in October 1921. A payment of £5,031 was made to 'Kate Collery, widow, and Annie Collery, Kathleen Collery, Mary Collery, Margaret Collery, Patrick Collery, Thomas Collery, and James Collery, minors, by the said Kate Collery, their mother and next friend.'[38] The payment included the sum of £2,000 in compensation for Mrs Collery and £3,031 for her seven 'surviving' children. The award was made by Judge Cusack at the Tralee Quarter Sessions.[39] Coincidentally, the compensation awards made to Catherine Collery and Agnes Beatrice Mackinnon appear on the same page of a ledger detailing the payments made to widows and families of deceased members of the forces of the Crown. Mrs Mackinnon, who did not have children, is listed as receiving an award of £9,500. Just five ledger entries above, the payment of £5,031 to Mrs Colley, a mother of seven children, is recorded and highlights the chasm in the way in which the bereaved were treated financially based on the rank their husbands held in the military regime. This is further evidenced in the payments made to the relatives of the other four men killed in the ambush. Whereas District Inspector McCaughey's widow received £4,800 in compensation, the payments to the families of constables McCormack, Cooney and Quirke were just £1,000, £470 and £360 respectively.[40]

Catherine Collery and her family lived at 65 Wolfe Tone Street in Limerick city. Catherine died on 16 November 1971.[41] A report on her passing recorded that she was 'a member of a highly esteemed and widely respected family. She was of a very quiet and retiring disposition but nevertheless enjoyed a wide circle of friends. An exemplary mother, she was a devout Catholic, a neighbour whose charity knew no bounds and at all times was most Christian in her outlook.'[42] Her son Fr James Collery, a six-month-old baby on the day of the Ballymacandy Ambush, celebrated his mother's Requiem Mass, having returned from his parish in Nairobi where he was a Spiritan missionary. After the funeral at St Michael's Church in Limerick, Catherine Collery made a final journey to Milltown and was laid to rest beside her husband in Killagha Abbey. Coincidentally, a few metres away, in the same burial ground lies John Carroll of Kilderry, one of the members of Fianna Éireann who scouted the roads and fields around the site of the ambush in 1921. Opponents in warfare, James Collery and John Carroll lie close by in death in the peaceful surrounds of the ruins of the Abbey of Our Lady of Bello Loco beneath the distant hills of Fybough and Cathair Con Rí.

James Collery is commemorated at the National Memorial Arboretum in Staffordshire, England.[43] Known as 'The Beat', an avenue of horse-chestnut trees includes a tree dedicated to each of the United Kingdom's police forces over the years. One of the plaques erected in the memorial garden reads: 'Dedicated to James Christopher Collery, Sergeant, Royal Irish Constabulary, shot dead with four other officers, Castlemaine, Co. Kerry, 1st June 1921, aged 45.'

Rita (Margaret Frances) Collery, one of James and Catherine's daughters, lived in Limerick until her death on St Stephen's Day in 1999. A woman from Milltown recounted a visit she paid to Rita at her home in the 1990s. The woman was seeing a friend in the city who told her that she lived near Rita Collery who had been born and raised in Milltown. They paid a visit and introduced themselves to Rita. Amid talk of Milltown, Rita became upset. 'I never want to hear of that place again,' she remarked. Memories of the day her father died, when Rita was not yet eight years old, remained emotive. The last time she saw her father, she told her visitors, he was lying in repose before the altar at the Sacred Heart Church under the vigil being maintained by Fr O'Sullivan. The young Rita bowed her head but noticed something lying on her father's chest. It was a parcel containing a present he had bought for her earlier that day in Tralee.[44]

POSTSCRIPT

'THEY ARE THE FELLOWS
THAT PUT US HERE'

L ocal folklore and oral histories, by their very nature, evolve and are often augmented and embellished for dramatic effect as the stories pass down from one generation to the next. The popular tales and reminiscences of Ballymacandy are no different in that respect, nor are they dissimilar to recollections and anecdotes about any of the other countless ambushes and skirmishes of the War of Independence across the island of Ireland, which now form part of our societal and community memory of this epochal phase of the tortuous journey towards independence.

One such story concerns a visit to Milltown many years after the Ballymacandy Ambush by one of those who had survived the attack. According to the tale, the unidentified Englishman and his wife were holidaying in Kerry in the late 1960s and he decided to show his wife the location where he had escaped the clutches of the IRA decades before. Visiting a local hostelry in Milltown, the couple were coaxed by the publican – with the typical diplomacy and interrogatory skills of any rural Irish vintner – to tell him more about themselves and where they had come from. Though initially apprehensive about revealing that he had been a member of the Black and Tans in the locality in the early 1920s and that he had been a survivor of the ambush at Ballymacandy, he must have felt sufficiently at ease to make that very revelation. Time had moved on, this was all in the past and the publican seemed like an understanding and decent sort of a fellow who wouldn't have drawn this disclosure to the attention of the other customers in the bar.

'Do you know something?' said the publican, 'there is a man still alive over the road near Castlemaine and he was involved in that ambush too. His name is Dan Mulvihill and I'm sure he'd love to meet you.' Offering directions to Mulvihill's home at Brackhill, the publican assured the retired Tan that bygones were bygones and, sure, wouldn't it be a way to bury the hatchet of those terrible times?

Suitably reassured and plucking up the courage to call unannounced to the home of one of the instigators of the ambush in which he had almost died, the former Black and Tan made the short journey to Brackhill with his wife. A knock on the door went without response. Mulvihill was not home at the time. On the following Sunday, on the way to Mass in Milltown, the peace-keeping publican bumped into the ex-IRA man. He told Mulvihill about his midweek customer. 'There was a man around during the week looking to meet you, Dan.'

'Oh yes, and who was he?'

'He was into the pub. Wasn't he one of the Tans ye ambushed in '21 and I told him to call over to see you. Did you not meet him?'

'I did not. Just as well. I'd have shot the bastard.'

Whether folklore or fact, the story does appear to have at least some basis in real events. According to Denis Sugrue, writing under the name 'Milltowner' in *The Kerryman* in 1971, such a visitor did come to the locality all those years after the ambush at Ballymacandy. Sugrue recalled:

> An interesting aftermath happened two years ago [1969] when two English visitors, a man and his wife arrived here to visit the scene of the ambush. He was last in the locality in 1921 and was one of the ambushed party that day. He informed the writer that in the thick of the fight he escaped over the ditch and concealed himself in an old furze-covered hole on the railway side of the road where he remained until all was over and made his way through the fields to Killorglin.[1]

Dan Mulvihill's fervent remarks on the way to Sunday Mass, whether real or imagined, can be attributed to his enduring, lifelong belief in republicanism and are indicative of the sentiments the elders of the Old IRA held dear even as the Republic of Ireland took its peaceful place among the nations of the earth. The republican ideals epitomised by Dan Mulvihill were not ones which always had majority support in the state they had fought to create, not least during a time when a bitter sectarian war was killing thousands in Northern Ireland. For Mulvihill and his surviving contemporaries from the War of Independence, the IRA campaign which grew from the civil-rights movement and the emergence of a new IRA north of the border in the late 1960s represented a seamless continuation of the battle in which he and his comrades had been involved decades before. For Mulvihill, the republic of the late 1960s abandoned the Six Counties at their time of greatest need. 'The North came out and we left them down. We stood idly by. The first in all our history that we pulled back. They asked for arms to defend themselves and could not give them.'[2]

Dan Mulvihill hitched his political wagon to Fianna Fáil, in the years after the revolution. At the general election in 1965, for example, he signed the nomination papers of Timothy 'Chub' O'Connor of Killorglin, another Old IRA veteran and Fianna Fáil TD for Kerry South between 1961 and 1981.[3] De Valera's party represented, for the majority of anti-Treatyites, the most obvious political exposition of their aspirations for a fully united Ireland and the achievement of the objectives for which they had fought. But like many of his contemporaries, Mulvihill remained active in the IRA, despite its prohibition by de Valera in the 1930s in his attempts to widen the political appeal of his party. Mulvihill was also briefly a member of Saor Éire, a socialist republican group headed up by the radical IRA leader Peadar O'Donnell.[4] In 1938 Mulvihill was given the honour by the Minister for Defence, Frank Aiken, of raising the Irish national flag at Spike Island in Cork on the occasion of the taking over of the Cork Harbour Defences – one of the so-called Treaty Ports – from the British, and is pictured with senior Fianna Fáil figures at the ceremony including Aiken, Éamon de Valera and James Ryan.[5]

Loyalty to Fianna Fáil and the party of de Valera was not always unquestioning or absolute, however. In December 1979 Dan Mulvihill wrote to the local Fianna Fáil TD, Timothy 'Chub' O'Connor. The letter proves that even decades after the contentious payments to the survivors and families of those connected with the rebellion had been largely dealt with, there remained a residual disappointment and anger at the way in which the state had treated those who fought to bring it into being. The then government, led by the new Taoiseach Charles Haughey and of which Chub was a backbencher, was considering a pay increase for ministers, something which prompted Mulvihill to write to his Old IRA comrade:

> Dear Chub,
>
> I was looking at the Paper today and I saw about the Ministerial [pay] rises. I got a Dead Fit of laughing. Out of a thousand, they took three hundred and fifty off me. I want you to do the following for me. Go to Bobby Molloy [Minister for Defence] and say to him is it a fact that you are taxing what's left of the old I.R.A. They are all over eighty. I did not know this and I thought it had been done away with some years ago. If it is true, do you mind tabling a question on it, now that ye are getting a rise yourselves. They are the fellows that put us here. I think the people of the country will be interested to hear about it.[6]

Dan Mulvihill died on 9 January 1985, one of the oldest surviving participants in the Ballymacandy Ambush. The aspiration of this book has been not only to tell the stories of the ordinary men and women, like Mulvihill, who took part in the epochal events on a country road in rural Kerry a century ago – be they RIC, Auxiliary, Black and Tan, IRA or civilian – but also to enable their stories to be told in their own words: through their accounts, letters, statements, notes, maps, diaries and other material and by reading and hearing what they had to say. They – the dead, the bereaved, the survivors, their families and the assailants – might not have received sufficient, or often any, recognition or financial recompense for the hardships they often endured in later life but that their story is being told a century later might, I hope, act as some compensation in itself.

A century on, the War of Independence continues to infuse our politics and divide opinion, albeit to a gradually decreasing extent. The eminent historian of the period Charles Townshend remarked that the significance of the Anglo-Irish War depends partly on where we view it from.[7] I wondered, as I delved into the story of Dan Mulvihill, James Collery and countless others, what perspective I was viewing things from. My only aspiration in approaching the subject of the Ballymacandy Ambush was to view it from a single, simple and uncomplicated vantage point, from across the fields at my home, and to imagine and recreate what happened in the blistering sunshine that momentous day in the townland of Ballymacandy.

APPENDIX I:
LIST OF PARTICIPANTS IN THE BALLYMACANDY AMBUSH, 1 JUNE 1921

*S*ources for this list include Brigade Activity Reports, pension applications held in the Military Archives, witness statements in the Bureau of Military History, lists provided by Dan Mulvihill and others as well as other information provided to the author.

Milltown Company, 6th Battalion, Kerry No.2 Brigade
Thomas O'Connor, Milltown (Officer Commanding)
Daniel Mulvihill, Brackhill, Castlemaine (Adjutant)
John [Jack] Flynn, Brackhill, Castlemaine
James Cronin, Brackhill, Castlemaine
Daniel Cronin, Brackhill, Castlemaine
Michael Galvin, Brackhill, Castlemaine
Denis Dowd, Brackhill, Castlemaine
James Barrett, Woodville, Milltown
Edward Barrett, Woodville, Milltown
Timothy Brick, Woodville, Milltown

Denis Quirke, Lyre, Milltown
Michael Scully, Dungeel, Killorglin
Mossie Casey, Ballinoe, Milltown
Michael Casey, Ballinoe, Milltown
John Cronin, Brackhill, Castlemaine
Edward Flynn, Brackhill, Castlemaine

Keel Company, 2nd Battalion, Kerry No.2 Brigade
Bryan O'Brien, Keel House, Castlemaine
James Daly, Annagh, Castlemaine
Michael Flynn, Annagh, Castlemaine
William Nagle, Ardcanaught, Castlemaine
John Kerrisk, Ardcanaught, Castlemaine
Owen [surname illegible], Gurtanedin, Castlemaine
Patrick Dowd, Ross, Castlemaine
Dan Foley, Shanakill, Castlemaine
Denis Foley, Shanakill, Castlemaine
Timothy Foley, Shanakill, Castlemaine
Timothy Flynn, Shanakill, Castlemaine
Michael O'Brien, Shanakill, Castlemaine
Timothy Foley, Ballyarkane, Castlemaine
Francis Lehane, Caherfilane, Castlemaine
Con Hanafin, White Gate, Castlemaine
William Myles, White Gate, Castlemaine
John McKenna, Gortanedin, Castlemaine
Patrick Dwyer, Castledrum, Castlemaine
Thomas P. Corcoran, Boolteens, Castlemaine
Dan Duggan, Ardcanaught, Castlemaine
John O'Dowd, Michigan, USA

Daniel Neill, Ardcanaught, Castlemaine
Thomas Shanahan, Fybough, Castlemaine

Kiltallagh Company, 2nd Battalion, Kerry No.2 Brigade
Alexander Mason, O/C, Kiltallagh (Officer Commanding)
William Burke, Ballygamboon
Thomas Knightly, Clounlassa
Michael O'Sullivan, Kiltallagh
Thomas McLoughlin, Aubee
John O'Brien, Connavoola
James Flynn, Brackhill
Jeremiah Daly, Castlemaine
Timothy Leary, Castlemaine

'A' Company, Tralee, 1st Battalion, Kerry No.1 Brigade
Thomas O'Connor
Billy Mullins
Jerry Myles
Billy Myles
Paddy Paul Fitzgerald
Michael O'Leary
Jeremiah (Jerry) 'Unkey' O'Connor
Donnchadha (Denis) O'Donoghue
Eugene Hogan
John L. O'Sullivan
Jerry Cronin
Michael Fleming
Michael (Mick) McMahon
Dan Jeffers

'B' Company, Tralee, 1st Battalion, Kerry No.1 Brigade
Dan Keating, Ballygamboon, Castlemaine

'D' Company, Tralee, 1st Battalion, Kerry No.1 Brigade
Joe Sugrue
'Big' Dan O'Sullivan

Castlegregory Company, 4th Battalion, Kerry No.1 Brigade
Tadhg Brosnan
Michael Duhig
Dan Rohan
Jimmy Daly

Farmers' Bridge Company, 1st Battalion, Kerry No.1 Brigade
Johnny O'Connor (Connor)

Scouts/outpost duty
John Heffernan, Captain, Callinafercy Company, 6th Battalion,
Kerry No.2 Brigade
George Nagle, Ballygamboon, D Company, Tralee, Kerry No.1
Brigade

Milltown/ Castlemaine members of Fianna Éireann
William Keane, Meanus, Castlemaine (Chief Scout)
Timothy O'Leary, Castlemaine
Daniel Moriarty, Castlemaine
Patrick Sullivan, Castlemaine
John Sullivan, Castlemaine
Edward McKenna, Milltown

John Carroll, Kilderry
Michael Casey
Bernard Daly, Castlemaine
James Mason, Castlemaine
Edward Hanafin, Ballymacandy
J. Slattery
Patrick Daly, Knockbrack
Timothy Teahan, Ballyfinnane
Richard McCarthy, Castlemaine
James Breen, Knockbrack

'H' Company, Fianna Éireann, Tralee
Jeremiah O'Shea, Clahane
Patrick Horan, Clahane
Cornelius Gorman, Clahane
John J. Foley, Clahane
John P. Foley, Clahane
James Foley, Clahane
Daniel Hanafin, Clahane
Matthew O'Shea, Clahane
Denis Leen, Clahane
Maurice Leen, Clahane
Edmond Sweeney, Clahane
Ulick Barrett, Clahane
Denis Foley, Clahane
Con Horan, Clahane
Thomas O'Connor, Clahane
Denis O'Connor, Clahane
Thomas Breen, Clahane
Jack Egan, Ballydunlea

Thomas Egan, Ballydunlea

Thomas Enright, Clahane

Edward Knightly, Bridge Street

A list contained in the Brigade Reports of the Military Archives also lists members of the Firies Company, 2nd Battalion, Kerry No.2 Brigade. It is noted that they were 'late for ambush':

Thomas Woods

Thomas O'Donoghue

Bill Donoghue

Jerry Flynn

Jim Riordan

Patrick Riordan

Batt Riordan

Peter Costelloe

Denis Scully

Ned Horan

Jack Brosnan

Con Sullivan

Neilus Curtin

Patrick Casey

Denis Breen

Charlie Breen

Daniel Spring

Michael Griffin

Bill Kerris

APPENDIX II:
MEMBERS OF MILLTOWN DISTRICT COUNCIL OF CUMANN NA MBAN, JULY 1921[1]

'A' Company, 6th Battalion, Kerry No.2 Brigade
Mary (May) Allman (O/C)
Nellie Corcoran (1st Lieutenant)
Kathleen Barrett (2nd Lieutenant)
Maggie Slattery
Kathy Healy
Annie Cronin
Mary Corcoran
Katie Mulvihill
Bridie Cronin
Kathy Heffernan
Julia Corcoran
Julia Healy
Kate McKenna
Maggie Spillane
Nell Scully
Kathy Scully

Nellie Langford
Margaret Scully
Mary B. Scully
Nellie Slattery
Nora Cronin
Kathy Connor
Maggie Carroll
Nora Sullivan
Alice Langford
Kathy Allman
Kate Daly
Minnie Keating
Bridie Mulvihill
Mary Coakley
Teresa McCarthy
Nora McGillycuddy
Hanna McKenna
Nora Flynn
Mary Sullivan
Julia Clifford

ACKNOWLEDGEMENTS

A story like this one does not get told without the generosity and assistance of many individuals, especially the descendants of those involved in the events. I am deeply grateful to so many of them.

Niall Lucey provided a copy of the reminiscences of Dan Mulvihill, which had been in the possession of his late father, Paul Lucey, whose own father Con Lucey of Caragh Lake, my wife's grand-uncle, was involved in the revolution and who fought beside and knew the men who led the ambush at Ballymacandy. The testimony of Dan Mulvihill, compiled in the late 1970s, was also held by his grand-nephew Shane Mulvihill as well as Stephen Rae and the late Liam Crowley of Killorglin who sadly passed away while this book was being written. I am grateful to Stephen Rae, grandson of Intelligence Officer with the Kerry No.1 Brigade Steve Rae, who provided a recording of an interview he and his father, David, completed with Dan Mulvihill in 1984, as well as an interview with Ned Horan of the Firies IRA. The tapes have been donated to the Kerry Library Archives.

Harry and Mary O'Neill provided crucial details on Mary's grandfather, Sergeant James Collery, which help to bring his story to life, as well as many images and other material. Relatives including Marian Burke, Oliver Mason, Kay Groves, Gillian

Sheehan, Pamela Sheehan, Fintan Quill, Carmel Quill, Willie Murphy, Mary Murphy, Seán Breen, John Hannafin, Dermot Cotter, John Lucey, Mary O'Sullivan, Diarmuid O'Keeffe, Eileen Dowd, Catherine Brick and Nell Kelliher also provided information, anecdotes and photographs in many cases. Thanks also to Sarah Caridia, Martin Moore, Mary Prendergast and Brendan Griffin TD for assistance and information.

Tommy O'Connor, Eamon Browne and the staff of Kerry Library as well as the staff of the University College Dublin Archives, the Military Archives, Kilmainham Gaol and the National Library were most helpful as was Helen O'Carroll of Kerry County Museum who provided access to a copy of Con Casey's unpublished memoir. Thanks also to Stephen Thompson and the Killorglin Archive Society for providing images and information.

Local historians Dr John Knightly and Thomas O'Sullivan provided a wealth of important information and insights. I am grateful to John for providing extracts of the diaries and correspondence of Major Leeson Marshall of Callinafercy and for reading the manuscript. Thomas O'Sullivan provided the recollections of his father, Thomas 'Totty' O'Sullivan, the lyrics of a song written about the ambush and other important anecdotal detail. Another local historian, Pat McKenna, also provided useful information. My cousin Bernard Cronin, outside whose home the ambush occurred, assisted with vital parts of the jigsaw and potential sources of information.

I would like to thank Gordon Revington, with whom I published a book on the county's political history in 2018, for reading a draft and offering important comments. I am very grateful to Dr Mary McAuliffe of UCD, with whom Bridget

McAuliffe and I co-edited a book on Kerry's role in the Easter Rising, for writing the foreword to this book.

I am extremely grateful to Conor Graham and his colleagues at Merrion Press for showing interest in this story and for encouraging and enabling me to share it with a wide audience. I thank all of them for their customary enthusiasm and professionalism.

Finally, I would like to thank my ever-encouraging wife Cecelia and my wonderful children, Peadar, Neasa and Aodhán, for their patience and support in indulging my enduring fascination with history. This book is dedicated to them.

ENDNOTES

Introduction

1 Cited by Diarmaid Ferriter, 'How 1920 unfolded' in supplement to the *Irish Times* on 1920, 3 June 2020.
2 Tomás Mac Conmara, *The Time of the Tans: An Oral History of the War of Independence in County Clare* (Mercier Press, 2019), p. 26.
3 Ferriter, 'How 1920 unfolded', *Irish Times*, 3 June 2020.

Preface

1 'Unlikely ambush position was deliberately chosen near Castlemaine' by Edward Gallagher in *With the IRA in the Fight for Freedom* (Mercier Press, 2010), p. 414. IRA member Dan Mulvihill later claimed that the summer of 1921 was the 'hottest weather I ever remember'; 'Recollections of Dan Mulvihill', unpublished, p. 11, kindly provided to the author by Niall Lucey, and hereinafter referred to as 'Recollections of Dan Mulvihill'.
2 Fr Thomas Egan (ed.), *Milltown Parish: A Centenary Celebration* (*Leinster Leader*, 1994), pp. 54–8.
3 Ibid. p. 56.
4 *Kerry Reporter*, 21 November 1925.
5 'Memories of the Ballymacandy Ambush by Milltowner', *The Kerryman*, 5 June 1971.
6 'Memories of a Milltown Ambush', Denis Sugrue, *The Kerryman*, 19 April 1983 (provided by Harry O'Neill).
7 'Milltowner', *The Kerryman*, 5 June 1971.
8 Sugrue, 'Memories of a Milltown Ambush'.
9 'Milltowner', *The Kerryman*, 5 June 1971.

Chapter One

1 T. Ryle Dwyer, *Tans, Terrors and Troubles: Kerry's Real Fighting Story, 1913–1923* (Mercier Press, 2001), pp. 126–7.
2 See Bridget McAuliffe, Mary McAuliffe and Owen O'Shea (eds), *Kerry 1916: Histories and Legacies of the Easter Rising – A Centenary Record* (Irish Historical Publications, 2016), pp. 113–20.

3   Martin Moore, *The Call to Arms: Tom McEllistrim and the Fight for Irish Freedom in Kerry* (An Gabha Beag, 2016), p. 27.

4   Jeremiah Murphy, *When Youth Was Mine* (Mentor Books, 1998), p. 125.

5   Donal J. O'Sullivan, *The Irish Constabularies 1822–1922: A Century of Policing in Ireland* (Brandon, 1999), *passim*, and J. Anthony Gaughan, *The Memoirs of Constable Jeremiah Mee R.I.C.* (Mercier Press, 1975), p. 200.

6   John Reynolds, *46 Men Dead: The Royal Irish Constabulary in County Tipperary, 1919–22* (The Collins Press, 2016), p. 15.

7   Richard Abbott, *Police Casualties in Ireland 1919–1922* (Mercier Press, 2019 edition), pp. 17–18.

8   O'Sullivan, *Irish Constabularies*, p. 291.

9   Sinéad Joy, *The IRA in Kerry 1916–1921* (The Collins Press, 2005), p. 29.

10   Fergal Keane, *Wounds: A Memoir of War and Love* (William Collins, 2017), p. 36.

11   Jim Herlihy, *The Royal Irish Constabulary* (Four Courts Press, 2016), p. 85.

12   The name is misspelt is some sources as 'Colleary'.

13   Information on the Collery family kindly provided by Harry and Mary O'Neill.

14   Elizabeth Malcolm cited by David M. Leeson, 'The Royal Irish Constabulary, the Black and Tans and the Auxiliaries' in John Crowley, Donal Ó Driscreoil, Mike Murphy and John Borgonovo (eds), *Atlas of the Irish Revolution* (Cork University Press, 2017), p. 372.

15   Service records of Royal Irish Constabulary, HO184/1-43 and HO184/45-48, British National Archives.

16   Census 1911, census.nationalarchives.ie.

17   Herlihy, *Royal Irish Constabulary*, p.160.

18   Egan, *Milltown Parish*, p. 64.

19   Herlihy, *Royal Irish Constabulary*, p. 92.

20   The 1911 Census lists four Collerys at Main Street, Milltown, including James, Catherine (30), Annie (2) and a baby, Catherine.

21   Pat McKenna, *Gwin for the Blue: a Milltown memoir* (Milltown, 2017), p. 38.

22   D.M. Leeson, *The Black and Tans: British Police and Auxiliaries in the Irish War of Independence* (Oxford University Press, 2011), p. 4; O'Sullivan, *Irish Constabularies*, p. 300.

23   Abbott, *Police Casualties*, p. 9.

24   O'Sullivan, *Irish Constabularies*, p. 299.

25   Abbott, *Police Casualties*, p. 83.

26   Cormac K.H. O'Malley and Tim Horgan (eds), *The Men Will Talk to Me: Kerry Interviews by Ernie O'Malley* (Mercier Press, 2012), p. 67.

27   Abbott, *Police Casualties*, p. 81.

28   Leeson, *Black and Tans*, p. ix.

29   'RIC historian Jim Herlihy has claimed that 883 Black and Tans were Irish-born and 126 Auxiliaries were Irish', *Irish Times*, 1 January 2020.

30   Keane, *Wounds*, p. 105.
31   *With the IRA in the Fight for Freedom*, p. 22.
32   Leeson, *Black and Tans*, p. 223.
33   William Sheehan, *British Voices: From the Irish War of Independence 1918–1921* (The Collins Press, 2007), p. 1.
34   Joy, *IRA in Kerry*, p. 99.
35   Keane, *Wounds*, p. 106.
36   Herlihy, *Royal Irish Constabulary*, p. 134.
37   Paul O'Brien, *Havoc: The Auxiliaries in Ireland's War of Independence* (The Collins Press, 2017), p. 29.
38   Murphy, *When Youth Was Mine*, p. 134–5.
39   Leeson, *Black and Tans*, p. 137; Herlihy, *Royal Irish Constabulary*, p. 107.
40   Keane, *Wounds*, p. 145.
41   Mac Conmara, *The Time of the Tans*, p. 30.
42   *Killarney Echo and South Kerry Chronicle*, 14 August 1920.

Chapter Two

1   Bureau of Military History (BMH), Witness Statement (WS) 938, Dan Mulvihill.
2   Ibid.
3   Recollections of Dan Mulvihill, p. 14; for more on the Battle of Ballyeagh see Seán Moraghan, *Days of the Blackthorn: Faction Fighting in Kerry* (Mercier Press, 2020), Chapter Three.
4   Census 1901 and Census 1911.
5   Recollections of Dan Mulvihill, p. 1; interview of Dan Mulvihill by David and Stephen Rae, 1984, reproduced with the kind permission of Stephen Rae.
6   Many Kerry men – including republican TDs like Tomás Ó Donnchú and Denis Daly from Cahersiveen – were drawn towards the London branches of the Gaelic League, the GAA and the IRB, while they were in London in their youth and before they returned to Ireland to join the armed struggle.
7   BMH, WS 938, Dan Mulvihill.
8   Recollections of Dan Mulvihill, p. 2; interview of Dan Mulvihill by David and Stephen Rae, 1984, reproduced with the kind permission of Stephen Rae.
9   Dwyer, *Tans, Terror and Troubles*, p. 13.
10   John Borgonovo, 'Army Without Banners: The Irish Republican Army, 1920–21', *Atlas of the Irish Revolution*, p. 390.
11   Map of Kerry IRA brigades and companies, *Atlas of the Irish Revolution* p. 545. The 6th Battalion was part of the Kerry No.1 Brigade until the spring of 1921 when it transferred to Kerry No.2.
12   Tom O'Connor interview in O'Malley and Horgan (eds), *The Men Will Talk to Me*, p. 146.

13 Tim Horgan, *Fighting for the Cause: Kerry's Republican Fighters* (Merrion Press, 2018), p. 251.
14 BMH, WS 1,067, Daniel Healy.
15 'In a remarkable twist of fate, Hurley was buried right beside Collins' brother Seán in Clonakilty in 1965, both men having made peace with each in the years after the bitter and divisive Civil War'; *Irish Examiner*, 2 February 2015.
16 Recollections of Dan Mulvihill, p. 2.
17 List compiled by Dan Mulvihill in the Brigade Activity Report, 'A7, 2 Kerry Brigade, 1 Southern Division', Military Archives, Cathal Brugha Barracks, Dublin.
18 For more on Jack Flynn, see Owen O'Shea and Gordon Revington, *A Century of Politics in the Kingdom: A County Kerry Compendium* (Merrion Press, 2018), pp. 51–61.
19 At the time of the death of Jack Flynn's mother, Hanoria Flynn, in 1940, it was noted that she had 'a disturbed and worried time during the Anglo-Irish War. Again and again, her home was raided by Crown Forces in search of her son', *The Kerryman*, 27 April 1940.
20 BMH, WS 938, Dan Mulvihill.
21 Joy, *IRA in Kerry*, p. 126.
22 Ibid. p. 105.
23 Borgonovo, 'Army Without Banners', *Atlas of the Irish Revolution*, p. 399.
24 Recollections of Dan Mulvihill, p. 3.
25 Negley Farson, *The Way of a Transgressor* (Edward Gaskell Publishers, 2001), p. 263.
26 Recollections of Dan Mulvihill, p. 3.
27 Cal McCarthy, *Cumann na mBan and the Irish Revolution* (Collins Press, 2007), p. 28.
28 Ibid. p. 155 and *Atlas of the Irish Revolution*, p. 407.
29 Letter dated 3 March 1941 in support of pension application of Mary Sheehan, Castledrum, Castlemaine; Military Service Pensions Collection, MSPC/34/REF7773, Military Archives.
30 Milltown District Council of Cumann na mBan, 6th Battalion, Kerry No.2 Brigade, MSPC/CMB/21, Military Archives.
31 Pension application of Margaret Slattery-Houlihan, MSP/34/REF14366, Military Archives.
32 Ibid.
33 Pension application of Annie J. Cronin, MSP/34/REF59978, Military Archives.
34 Letter from Dan Mulvihill to Pensions Board, 19 October 1940; pension application of Mary Sheehan; MSPC/34/REF7773, Military Archives.
35 Pension application of Margaret Slattery-Houlihan, MSP/34/REF14366, Military Archives.

36   Summary of sworn evidence given before the Interviewing Officers by Mrs Mary Ann Duggan on 7 January 1941, and agreed by her; Pension application of Mary Ann Duggan, MSP/34/REF13876, Military Archives.
37   Letter from Capt. John Heffernan, Callinafercy, Milltown, Co. Kerry to the Pensions Board, Pension application of Mary Ann Duggan.
38   Pension applications of Nora Corcoran, MSP/34/REF6698 and Nellie Foley MSP/34/REF6638, Military Archives.
39   According to the pension application of John Heffernan, the barracks was burned and abandoned in July 1919; MSP/34/REF10816, Military Archives.
40   Pension application of Nora Corcoran.
41   Letter from Bryan O'Brien in support of the application for a military pension by Nora Corcoran, 25 May 1940; pension application of Nora Corcoran.
42   Pension application of Mary (May) O'Sullivan, MSP/34/REF8597.
43   Pension application of Mary Sheehan.
44   Ibid.

Chapter Three

1   'Milltowner', *The Kerryman*, 5 June 1971.
2   Patrick O'Sullivan, *I Heard the Wild Birds Sing: A Kerry Childhood* (Anvil Books, 1991), p. 192 and Shelley Barber (ed.), *The Prendergast Letters: Correspondence from Famine-era Ireland* (University of Massachusetts Press, 2006), p. 7.
3   O'Sullivan, *I Heard the Wild Birds Sing*, p. 125.
4   In 1841 the population of Milltown was 797 people and in 1851 this had fallen to 485; O'Sullivan, *I Heard the Wild Birds Sing*, p. 128.
5   John Knightly, 'The Godfrey Family of Kilcoleman Abbey' (unpublished), p. 28.
6   Barber, *Prendergast Letters*, p. 18, 54.
7   *Kerry Sentinel*, 16 December 1884, cited in Donnacha Seán Lucey, *Land, Popular Politics and Agrarian Violence in Ireland, The Case of County Kerry 1872–86* (UCD Press, 2011), p. 133.
8   *Killarney Echo and South Kerry Chronicle*, 28 March 1914.
9   *Cork Examiner*, 17 October 1914.
10   *Kerry Weekly Reporter*, 22 November 1913.
11   *The Kerryman*, 14 February 1914.
12   Information courtesy of John Knightly.
13   *Kerry News*, 10 January 1919.
14   Information from Thomas O'Sullivan.
15   *Killarney Echo and South Kerry Chronicle*, 18 January 1919.
16   Brigade Activity Report, Kerry No.2 Brigade, Military Archives. The author of the report, Dan Mulvihill, noted 'I don't think he was injured.' Those

involved in the attack were all members of the Callinafercy Company including John P. Heffernan, Edward Langford, John J. Clifford, Jeremiah Clifford, Michael J. Clifford and Timothy J. Clifford.

17   John Knightly, p. 42 and O'Sullivan, *I Heard the Wild Birds Sing*, p. 136. The Crown Hotel is now Larkin's Bar and was previously owned by the O'Connor family.

18   Knightly, *Godfrey Family*, p. 42.

19   Ibid.

20   Diary of Major Markham Richard Leeson Marshall, 10 May 1921; Leeson Marshall Papers, private collection.

21   Information on Major Leeson Marshall kindly provided by John Knightly.

22   Valerie Bary, *Houses of Kerry* (Ballinakella Press, 1994), p. 61; information from John Knightly.

23   The only child of Major Leeson Marshall and Mabel Godfrey, May (later Mrs George Ruth) was raised by her grandmother, Lady Mary Cordelia Godfrey, at Kilcoleman Abbey.

24   O'Sullivan, *I Heard the Wild Birds Sing*, p. 87.

25   Information from John Knightly.

26   Pension application of John Heffernan, MSP/34/REF10816, Military Archives.

27   BMH, WS 1,000, James Cronin.

28   Denis Sugrue, *Milltown: Memories of Other Days* (1984), p. 25.

29   Ibid. p. 27.

30   Patrick Long, 'Smyth, Gerald Bryce Ferguson' in *Dictionary of Irish Biography*, www.dib.cambridge.org.

31   BMH, WS 379, Jeremiah Mee; J. Anthony Gaughan, The Memoirs of Constable Jeremiah Mee RIC (Mercier Press, 2012), passim; 'The Listowel Policy Mutiny, 1920, A Centenary Commemorative Exhibition,' www.kerrywritersmuseum.com.

32   Gaughan, *Jeremiah Mee*, p. 98.

33   Sometimes spelt O'Shea but listed as 'O'Shee' in many RIC records.

34   RIC Officers' Register, John Marcus Poer O'Shea, Royal Irish Constabulary Records; Hugh Montgomery-Massingberd, *Burke's Irish Family Records* (Burke's Peerage Ltd, 1976).

35   Brian Ó Conchubhair (ed.) *Kerry's Fighting Story 1916–1921* (Mercier Press, 2009), pp. 223–5 and Gaughan, *Jeremiah Mee*, pp. 264–6.

36   Gaughan, *Jeremiah Mee*, pp. 264–6.

37   Ibid. p. 266.

38   Ibid.

39   Long, 'Smyth, Gerald Bryce Ferguson', *Dictionary of Irish Biography*.

40   *Killarney Echo and South Kerry Chronicle*, 17 July 1920.

41   BMH, WS 1,181, Johnny O'Connor (usually referred to as Johnny Connor).

42   *Irish Times*, 21 August 1920; Horgan, *Fighting for the Cause*, p. 266. Daniel Allman died during the Headford Junction Ambush in 1921 and Charlie

Daly died in County Donegal during the Civil War in 1923. The RIC County Inspector's Report for Kerry for August 1920 claims that there were 'two attempts … to blow up Milltown old barracks' but this is the only known reference to more than one such attempt; RIC County Inspector's Report, October 1920, POS/8552, National Library of Ireland.

43   Bertie Scully in *The Men Will Talk to Me*, p. 155; RIC County Inspector's Report for Kerry for October 1920, POS/8552, National Library of Ireland.

44   RIC County Inspector's Report for Kerry for October 1920.

45   Bertie Scully in *The Men Will Talk to Me*, p. 157.

46   Map showing the location of RIC barracks in Ireland in January 1919 and January 1921, *Atlas of the Irish Revolution*, p. 377.

47   *Kerry People*, 25 September 1920.

48   *Kerry People*, 9 October 1920.

49   See, for example, 'The rarely spoken about violence suffered by women during the Irish revolution', *Irish Examiner*, 12 September 2017; *Cogadh ar Mhná* directed by Ciara Hyland, RTÉ/TG4, 2020.

50   RIC County Inspector's Report for Kerry for October 1920.

Chapter Four

1   Recollections of Dan Mulvihill, p. 5.

2   Ibid.

3   W.H. Kautt, *Ambushes and Armour: The Irish Rebellion* (Irish Academic Press, 2010), pp. 90–1.

4   Murphy, *When Youth Was Mine*, p. 133.

5   John Borgonovo, 'The IRA and the war', centenary supplement on 1920, *Irish Times*, 3 June 2020.

6   Recollections of Dan Mulvihill, p. 4.

7   Tom O'Connor in *The Men Will Talk to Me*, p. 137.

8   Brigade Activity Reports contained in the Military Archives and pension application of Cornelius 'Con' Lucey MSP/34/REF44763. Con Lucey's sister, Nora was a member of Cumann na mBan. According to the brigade records, among those 'paraded for the job' were Daniel Allman, Rockfield (Captain); Thomas Lyne; S. Hobbins and John Flynn, Kilbonane; James Doyle, Culeenymore; James Sullivan, Ballymalis; Thomas Brosnan, Lisaree; John Scully, Michael Scully and Dan P. Scully, Nauntinaun; John Scannell, Coolroe and Daniel Healy, Rockfield. Also involved were members of the Callinafercy company including John P. Heffernan, Michael J. Clifford, Jeremiah Clifford, Edward Langford, Maurice Harmon, John Clifford and John Sullivan. The 'outpost men' listed in the Military Archives files include Timothy J. Clifford, Timothy Sullivan, Jack Knightly, Daniel Sullivan, John D. Clifford, Michael Sullivan, John Kearin, Timothy Kearin and John Clifford.

9   BMH, WS 1,067, Daniel Healy.

10   *Cork Examiner*, 3 November 1920.

11   House of Commons Debates, 1 November 1920.

12   *Cork Examiner*, 6 November 1920.

13   Ibid.

14   Gregory 'Greg' Ashe in *The Men Will Talk to Me*, p. 121.

15   Bertie Scully in *The Men Will Talk to Me*, pp. 69–70.

16   *Cork Examiner*, 3 November 1920; BMH Daniel Healy; Seán Moraghan, *Puck Fair: A History* (The History Press, 2013), p. 69.

17   Patrick Houlihan, *Cast a Laune Shadow: Reminiscences of Life in Killorglin* (Killarney Printing Works, 1997), p. 100.

18   *Irish Independent* report reproduced in *The Kerry People*, 6 November 1920.

19   Correspondence with Bishop Charles O'Sullivan, 5 November 1918 and June 1921; Kerry Diocesan Archives, Diocesan Office, Killarney.

20   Major Leeson Marshall to his daughter May, 3 November 1920, Leeson Marshall Papers, private collection.

21   Diary of Major Leeson Marshall, 17 January 1921.

22   Note by Sir William Godfrey, November 1920 (Godfrey papers, private collection). A garnishee order, often in the form of a legal notice, is a common form of enforcing a debt to recover money.

23   Tom O'Connor in *The Men Will Talk to Me*, p. 137.

24   Information from John Knightly.

25   Information from Thomas O'Sullivan.

26   Pension application, Margaret Slattery-Houlihan, op cit.

27   Pension application, Amelia Mason, MSP/34/REF 56048, Military Archives.

28   Tom O'Connor in *The Men Will Talk to Me*, p. 137.

29   Information from sketch map drawn by Dan Mulvihill and included in the Brigade Activity Report in the Military Archives.

30   See also Michael Connolly (ed.), *The Unquiet Grave: the development of Kerry's burial grounds through the ages* (Kerry County Council, 2012), pp. 128–30.

31   James Carmody, 'The Abbey of Killagha, Parish of Kilcoleman, County Kerry', *The Journal of the Royal Society of Antiquaries of Ireland* (Fifth Series, vol. 36, no. 3, 1906), pp. 285–96.

32   BMH, WS 938, Daniel Mulvihill. A full list of the participants in the Kilderry Ambush is contained in the Brigade Activity Reports in the Military Archives.

33   Information from sketch map drawn by Dan Mulvihill and included in the Brigade Activity Report in the Military Archives.

34   BMH, WS 1,067 Daniel Healy.

35   Prionnsias Breathnach, 'Creamery Attacks' in *Atlas of the Irish Revolution*, p. 555.

36   https://www.theirishstory.com/2012/11/06/the-siege-of-tralee-november-1-9-1920/ retrieved on 10 April 2020.

37   *Kerry People*, 14 May 1921.
38   House of Commons, 30 May 1921.
39   Con Casey memoirs, unpublished, p. 35, courtesy of Helen O'Carroll, Kerry County Museum.

Chapter Five

1   *Kerry People*, 8 January 1921.
2   Interview of Ned Horan by David and Stephen Rae, 1984, reproduced with the kind permission of Stephen Rae. Ned Horan was later a senator representing Clann na Talmhan.
3   Richard Bennett, *The Black and Tans* (Pen & Sword Military, 2010), p. 177.
4   Murphy, *When Youth Was Mine*, p. 148.
5   Joy, *IRA in Kerry*, p. 91.
6   Diary of Major Leeson Marshall, 27 February, 5 April, 27 April 1921.
7   RIC County Inspector Reports for Kerry for April and May 1921, POS/8554, National Library.
8   Tom O'Connor in *The Men Will Talk to Me*, p. 139.
9   Bertie Scully in *The Men Will Talk to Me*, p. 156. See also Thomas Earls Fitzgerald, '… the Killorglin town crowd were no good', *Nordic Irish Studies*, vol. 17, no. 2 (2018), pp. 185–202. According to Jimmy Cronin of Brackhill, the 'IRA had no friends in the town of Killorglin', BMH, WS 1,000, James Cronin.
10   *The Men Will Talk to Me*, p. 139, n. 20.
11   Moraghan, *Puck Fair*, pp. 65–7.
12   *The Kerryman*, 7 August 1920 and Moraghan, *Puck Fair*, p. 68.
13   BMH, WS 788, Seán 'Bertie' Scully.
14   Recollections of Dan Mulvihill, p. 6; BMH, WS 788, Sean 'Bertie' Scully; Tim Horgan, *Dying for the Cause: Kerry's Republican Dead* (Mercier Press, 2015), p. 344.
15   Bertie Scully observed that 'the scouting by the Killorglin scouts caused the whole catastrophe and the O.C.'s dependence on them led me to comment very bitterly on the abortive business as a whole', BMH, WS 788, Sean 'Bertie' Scully.
16   Horgan, *Dying for the Cause*, p. 343.
17   BMH, WS 788, Seán 'Bertie' Scully.
18   Recollections of Dan Mulvihill, p. 6.
19   Horgan, *Dying for the Cause*, p. 344.
20   BMH, WS 788, Seán 'Bertie' Scully.
21   Bertie Scully in *The Men Will Talk to Me*, p. 155.
22   Recollections of Dan Mulvihill, p. 6; *Kerry People*, 12 March 1921.
23   *Kerry People*, 19 March 1921.
24   Tom O'Connor in *The Men Will Talk to Me*, p. 132.
25   *Kerry People*, 19 March 1921.

26   Dwyer, *Tans, Terror and Troubles*, p. 25 and pp. 289–95.
27   Dan Mulvihill, 'Glenbeigh Ambush took place 50 years ago', *The Kerryman*, 1 May 1971.
28   List of IRA companies at Glenbeigh Ambush, Kerry No.1 Brigade Activity Report, Military Archives; Horgan, *Fighting for the Cause*, pp. 83–4.
29   RIC County Inspector's Report for Kerry for April 1921, POS/8554, National Library of Ireland.
30   Joy, *IRA in Kerry*, p. 69.
31   For a chronology of events during May 1921, see Dwyer, *Tans, Terror and Troubles*, p. 27.
32   RIC County Inspector's Report for Kerry for May 1921, POS/8554, National Library of Ireland.
33   Ibid.
34   Pension application of Edward Langford, MSP/34/REF16492, Military Archives.
35   *Irish Independent*, 25 May 1921.
36   *Freeman's Journal*, 4 June 1921.
37   *Freeman's Journal*, 1 and 4 June 1921.

Chapter Six

1   Teachta Dála or TD is the Irish language term for Member of Parliament.
2   https://voicesfromthedawn.com/caherconree retrieved on 12 August 2020.
3   Gallagher in *With the IRA in the Fight for Freedom*, p. 414.
4   RIC County Inspector's Report for Kerry for October 1920.
5   BMH, WS, 801, Billy Mullins.
6   RIC County Inspector's Report for Kerry for November 1920 (REF).
7   Information from David and Stephen Rae.
8   BMH, WS, 1,167 Michael O'Leary.
9   BMH, WS 1,011, Patrick Garvey.
10   Joy, *IRA in Kerry*, p. 51.
11   Bertie Scully in *The Men Will Talk to Me*, p. 157.
12   Letter from Jerry Myles, Castle Countess, Tralee, in support of application of Mary Ann Duggan; pension application of Mary Ann Duggan.
13   Murphy, *When Youth Was Mine*, p. 145.
14   BMH, WS 1,167, Michael O'Leary.
15   The six other TDs elected for Kerry in the 1921 general election were Austin Stack, Con Collins, Piaras Béaslaí, Edmond Roche, Fionán Lynch and James Crowley.
16   RIC County Inspector's Report for Kerry for May 1921.
17   Michael Hopkinson, *The Irish War of Independence* (Gill and Macmillan, 2004), p. 128.
18   Joy, *IRA in Kerry*, pp. 82–3.
19   BMH, WS 1,416, Tadhg Kennedy.

20 Recollections of Dan Mulvihill, p. 7.
21 Recollections of Dan Mulvihill, p. 9. Mulvihill claims that on leaving Brackhill, Liam Lynch asked him to join the IRA Divisional staff: 'I said I would. I thought it was the greatest thing that ever happened – to be asked.'
22 Hopkinson, *War of Independence*, p. 128.
23 Details of the Tralee IRA participants at Ballymacandy from various sources including Dwyer, *Tans, Terror and Troubles*, pp. 316–17.
24 Ibid. p. 324.
25 Tadhg Kennedy in *The Men Will Talk to Me*, p. 91.
26 Con Casey memoirs, p. 58.
27 See Billy Mullins, *Memoirs of Billy Mullins: Veteran of the War of Independence* (Kenno, 1983).
28 Mullins, *Memoirs*, p. 132.

Chapter Seven

1 Diarmaid Ferriter, *The Transformation of Ireland 1900–2000* (Profile Books, 2004), p. 227.
2 Pa Houlihan notes that the RIC barracks was previously located on Langford Street. After the establishment of the Free State, the barracks became the local headquarters of An Garda Síochána; see Houlihan, *Cast a Laune Shadow*, p. 58.
3 Census 1901, some sources mistakenly describe McCaughey as a native of County Monaghan.
4 Census 1901.
5 Abbott, *Police Casualties*, p. 316.
6 Medal card of McCaughey, Michael Francis, WO 372/12/192191, British National Archives, and Abbott, *Police Casualties*, p. 316; Eunan O'Halpin and Daithí Ó Corráin, *The Dead of the Irish Revolution* (Yale University Press, 2020), p. 456.
7 Some sources have referred to McCaughey as an Auxiliary but members of ADRIC were not usually assigned an RIC warrant number, which is provided for McCaughey in official records; O'Sullivan, *Irish Constabularies*, p. 310. Moreover, McCaughey joined the ranks before ADRIC was formed in the summer of 1920, which confirms his position as a member of the Black and Tans.
8 Bertie Scully in *The Men Will Talk to Me*, p. 156.
9 BMH, WS 788, Sean 'Bertie' Scully.
10 BMH, WS 1,079, Patrick P. Fitzgerald.
11 Leeson, *Black and Tans*, p. 28.
12 Sources for police identity numbers and other information from RIC Records held in the British National Archives and Jim Herlihy's book on the RIC, *The Royal Irish Constabulary*, passim.
13 Census 1911.

14   Census 1911.

15   *Irish Independent*, 8 June 1921.

16   Spelt as 'Quirk' in some of the records.

17   One source suggests that Quirke was from Clonakilty: O'Halpin and Ó Corráin, *The Dead of the Irish Revolution*, p. 456.

18   Letter from Major Leeson Marshall to his daughter May, 7 June 1921.

19   See Chapter Three.

20   Local historian Denis Sugrue claimed that Harvie was Scottish but this has not been verified; Sugrue, *Memories of Other Days*, p. 59.

21   Twomey is spelt as Toomey in some accounts.

22   File on inquiry into the death of Joe Taylor, WO 35/160, Royal Irish Constabulary Records, British National Archives.

23   BMH, WS 788, Seán 'Bertie' Scully.

24   *Cork Examiner*, 6 November 1920.

25   O'Malley and Horgan (eds), *The Men Will Talk to Me*, p. 121, n. 35.

26   See Chapter Three.

27   Evidence of Constable William Harvie at Court of Inquiry into events at Ballymacandy; Records of the Royal Irish Constabulary, British National Archives.

28   Information courtesy of Thomas O'Sullivan.

29   The name Bleach Road derived from a tradition of flax and linen production: the linen was bleached in the surrounding fields along the road.

30   The 'Pound Height' derived its name from the pound where seized animals were detained for non-payment of rent.

31   The 'Short Mountain' road is a narrow mountain road between Castlemaine and Tralee and often used a shortcut to and from Tralee.

32   Pension application of Katie Mulvihill, MSP/34/REF59896; BMH, WS 938, Daniel Mulvihill. The Caseys lived at Ardwanig, Milltown but their address or homeplace is usually referred to as Ballinoe.

33   Letter from Dan Mulvihill on pension file of Michael Casey, MSP/34/REF56399.

34   Pension application of Mary Riordan, *née* Casey, MSP/34/REF62133.

35   Letter of Dan Mulvihill on pension file of Michael Casey, MSP/34/REF56399.

36   Gallagher, *With the IRA in the Fight for Freedom*, p. 415.

37   BMH, WS 938, Daniel Mulvihill.

38   Recollections of Dan Mulvihill, p. 9.

39   BMH, WS 1,181, Johnny Connor.

40   BMH, WS 1,000, James Cronin; Tom O'Connor in *The Men Will Talk to Me*, p. 135.

41   Recollections of Dan Mulvihill, p. 11.

42   BMH, WS 1,000, James Cronin.

43   Horgan, *Dying for the Cause*, pp. 128–9.

44 Horgan, *Fighting for the Cause*, p. 75.
45 Gregory 'Greg' Ashe, *The Men Will Talk to Me*, p. 122.
46 Footnote on Michael Duhig in Horgan, *Fighting for the Cause*, p. 341.
47 Brigade Activity Reports, Military Archives.
48 Pension application of Nellie Foley.
49 Ibid.
50 Gallagher in *With the IRA in the Fight for Freedom*, p. 415.
51 Recollections of Dan Mulvihill, pp. 9–10.
52 Ibid. p. 9.
53 BMH, WS 788, Seán 'Bertie' Scully.
54 Recollections of Dan Mulvihill, p. 9.
55 List of members of Kiltallagh Company from the Brigade Activity Reports, Military Archives.
56 Horgan, *Dying for the Cause*, p. 263. In the Brigade report, McLoughlin is listed as '4 British Army, Lancaster [?]'
57 Diarmaid Fleming, 'Last Man Standing', *History Ireland*, vol. 16, no. 3 (May/June 2008).
58 BMH, WS 788, Seán 'Bertie' Scully. In his interview with Ernie O'Malley, Scully observed that 'a Tan, who had friends in C [Castlemaine], was told to "mind yourself when you are going in to Killorglin" for the friend must have known of the ambush position …'
59 Evidence of Constable William Harvie at Court of Inquiry.
60 Collins Papers, *IRA Intelligence reports on civilians accused of giving information to, and associating with, British Forces during War of Independence in counties Cork, Kerry, Waterford and Limerick*, IE-MA-CP-04-40, Military Archives.
61 Ibid.
62 Dan Mulvihill noted that the RIC 'decided they were dead safe as far as Milltown', Recollections of Dan Mulvihill, p. 10.
63 RIC County Inspector's Report for Kerry for April 1921, 9 May 1921.
64 Testimony of Constable William Harvie at Court of Inquiry

Chapter Eight

1 Information from Thomas O'Sullivan.
2 Census 1911.
3 Moore, *McEllistrim*, p. 28.
4 Marnie Hay, 'Na Fianna Éireann' in *Atlas of the Irish Revolution*, p. 173.
5 *The Kerryman*, 7 October 1911, 28 June 1913.
6 Information from Seán Breen, grandson of James Breen and John Hanafin, grand-nephew of Eddie Hanafin.
7 Map drawn by Dan Mulvihill on Ballymacandy Ambush, Brigade Activity Reports, Military Archives.
8 Information from John Knightly.

9   Gallagher in *With the IRA in the Fight for Irish Freedom*, p. 418.

10   Ibid.

11   W.H. Kautt, 'Ambushes in the War of Independence, 1919–21', in *Atlas of the Irish Revolution*, p. 409.

12   For the full list of those present at the ambush, see Appendix 1.

13   Bary, *Houses of Kerry*, p. 81.

14   BMH WS 1,189, Thomas O'Connor (Tralee).

15   BMS, WS 1,079, Patrick P. Fitzgerald.

16   BMS, WS 1,079, Patrick P. Fitzgerald and WS 938 Dan Mulvihill.

17   Gallagher, *With the IRA in the Fight for Irish Freedom*, p. 417.

18   BMH, WS 1,079, Patrick P. Fitzgerald.

19   BMH, WS 1,000, James Cronin.

20   BMS, WS 1,079, Patrick P. Fitzgerald.

21   Ibid.

22   BMH, WS 1,181, Johnny Connor.

23   Testimony of Dan Keating, cited in J.J. Barrett, *In the Name of the Game* (Dub Press, 1997), p. 60; Gallagher writes that O'Connor, 'armed with a grenade, lobs it accurately on the road, and the sergeant goes down riddled with shrapnel fragments', *With the IRA in the Fight for Freedom*, p. 419.

24   Bertie Scully in *The Men Will Talk to Me*, p. 157.

25   BMH, WS 1,000, James Cronin.

26   Ibid.

27   Pension application of Michael Casey.

28   Summary of Sworn Evidence given before Interviewing Officer by Michael Casey on 6 January 1942; pension application of Michael Casey.

29   Evidence of Constable William Harvie at Court of Inquiry.

30   Ibid.; Denis Sugrue, *Memories of Other Days*, p. 59.

31   Ibid.

32   Leeson, *Black and Tans*, pp. 139–40.

33   Gallagher, *With the IRA in the Fight for Freedom*, p. 419.

34   Recollections of Dan Mulvihill, p. 10.

35   Ibid.

36   BMH, WS 788, Sean 'Bertie' Scully. Greg Ashe of Lispole later recounted that at the ambush Mulvihill had 'a repeating shotgun and he let lash with it', *The Men Will Talk to Me*, p. 121.

37   BMH, WS 938, Daniel Mulvihill.

38   BMH, WS 1,079, Patrick P. Fitzgerald.

39   BMH, WS 1,079, Patrick P. Fitzgerald. In his witness statement, Billy Mullins claims it was £87.

40   Pension application of Thomas Corcoran, MSP/34/REF31668, Military Archives; pension application of Katie Mulvihill.

41   Ibid.

42   Summary of Sworn Evidence given before Interviewing Officer by Michael Casey on 6 January 1942; pension application of Michael Casey.

43 Information from Oliver Mason.
44 Diary of Major Leeson Marshall, 1 June 1921.
45 Ibid.
46 The author is grateful to John Knightly for references to this incident.
47 *Freeman's Journal*, 1 February 1921; *Cork Examiner*, 1 February 1921.
48 Diary of Major Leeson Marshall, 1 June 1921.

Chapter Nine

1 Diary of Major Leeson Marshall, 2 June.
2 Evidence of William Whinton at Court of Inquiry.
3 Whinton had been on duty in Milltown as far back as 1913. He lived with his wife Ellen (d. 1942) and their eight children. William died at his daughter's home in Tralee in 1953. They are interred in the grounds of the Church of Ireland in Milltown; Census 1911.
4 Whinton is listed in the 1911 Census as a sergeant at Milltown Barracks.
5 BMH, WS 1,000, James Cronin; information from John Knightly.
6 Evidence of William Whinton at Court of Inquiry.
7 Ibid.
8 Evidence of Dr Daniel Sheehan at Court of Inquiry.
9 Information courtesy of Tom Sheehan.
10 BMH, WS 1,765, Seán T. O'Kelly.
11 O'Sullivan, *I Heard the Wild Birds Sing*, p. 91; Bary, *Houses of Kerry*, p. 127.
12 *Killarney Echo and South Kerry Chronicle*, 17 July 1920.
13 'Milltowner', *The Kerryman*, 5 June 1971.
14 Pension application of Annie Cronin.
15 'Milltowner', *The Kerryman*, 5 June 1971.
16 *The Kerryman*, 2 October 1954.
17 Evidence of injuries sustained by Constable Joseph Cooney given to the Military Court of Inquiry.
18 BMH, WS 788, Sean 'Bertie' Scully.
19 Information from Collery family tree, courtesy of Harry and Mary O'Neill.
20 Diary of Major Leeson Marshall, 2 June 1921.
21 Evidence of William Whinton to Military Court of Inquiry.
22 Details from evidence given at the Military Inquiry.
23 Information from Thomas O'Sullivan.
24 McKenna, *Gwin for the Blue*, p. 41.
25 Evidence of William Whinton at Military Inquiry.
26 Evidence of Lt Frank Snoxell at Military Inquiry.
27 *Evening Echo*, 2 June 1921.
28 Evidence of Dr Daniel Sheehan at Military Inquiry.
29 Evidence of Lt Frank Snoxell at Military Inquiry.
30 Diary of Major Leeson Marshall, 2 June 1921.
31 Ibid.

Chapter Ten

1   Hargrave is listed in the 1911 Census at 15 Denny Street, Tralee. He attended the Church of Ireland Synod of the Diocese of Ardfert and Aghadoe in 1909 according to the *Kerry Evening Post* of 16 October 1909.
2   Dwyer, *Tans, Terror and Troubles*, pp. 302–3.
3   For more on the history of Ballymullen Barracks, see Robert Tangney, *The History of Ballymullen Barracks* (Tralee, 2014).
4   Evidence of Dr A.A. Hargrave at Military Inquiry.
5   'Memories of a Milltown Ambush' by Denis Sugrue, courtesy of Harry O'Neill.
6   Military Inquiry into the events at Ballymacandy, 3 June 1921, Royal Irish Constabulary Records, WO/35/153B/20, British National Archives.
7   By the time of his death, one of Sgt Collery's nine children, Agnes, had died. She contracted whooping cough and died four days before Christmas in 1915.
8   Diary of Major Leeson Marshall, 2 June 1921.
9   *Irish Independent*, 3 June 1921.
10 *Kerry People*, 11 June 1921.

Chapter Eleven

1   *Irish Independent*, 3 June 1921.
2   *Irish Times*, 3 June 1921.
3   *Times of London*, 3 June 1921.
4   *The Kerryman*, 3 June 1950.
5   Recollections of Dan Mulvihill, p. 11.
6   BMH, WS 788, Sean 'Bertie' Scully; Recollections of Dan Mulvihill, p. 10; pension application of Nellie Foley.
7   Recollections of Dan Mulvihill, p. 11.
8   *Evening Echo*, 8 June 1921.
9   Diary of Major Leeson Marshall, 4 June 1921.
10 Ibid.
11 *Irish Independent*, 8 June 1921; *Irish Times*, 8 June 1921.
12 *Evening Echo*, 8 June 1921; *Kerry People*, 11 June 1921.
13 Pension application of Annie Cronin.
14 Letter from Major Leeson Marshall to his daughter May, 20 June 1921.
15 Murphy, *When Youth Was Mine*, p. 149.
16 David M. Leeson, 'Reprisals' in *Atlas of the Irish Revolution*, p. 384.
17 *Kerry People*, 12 February 1921.
18 *Kerry People*, 14 May 1921.
19 *Kerry People*, 5 March 1921.
20 The *Kerry People* of 4 June 1921 reported: 'News reached Tralee that during Thursday night a farm house belonging to a man named Corcoran was

destroyed by fire at the Killorglin side of Milltown.' The *Irish Independent* of 16 June also reported that the house of a labourer, Thomas Corcoran of Knockavota, was destroyed by fire.

21   Diary of Major Leeson Marshall, 8 June 1921. In a letter to his daughter May, on 20 June, the major also recorded that he had been 'served with a notice that the place will be burnt if there are any burnings over the ambush'.

22   Tom O'Connor in *The Men Will Talk to Me*, p. 138.

23   Diary of Major Leeson Marshall, 10 June.

24   Leeson, 'Reprisals', p. 384.

25   *Kerry People*, 18 June 1921.

26   Leeson Marshall Papers, private collection. May Leeson Marshall (1891–1988) married George Anesley Ruth in 1924 and was known in the locality as Mrs Ruth.

27   BMH, WS 788, Seán 'Bertie' Scully.

28   *Evening Herald*, 2 July 2012

29   Information from Stephen Rae.

30   Tom O'Connor in *The Men Will Talk to Me*, p. 140.

31   *Evening Herald*, 2 July 2012.

32   BMH, WS 1,011, Patrick Garvey.

33   BMH, WS 1,167, Michael O'Leary.

34   Johnny O'Connor stated that 'Cahill in the C/W [Civil War] made a dugout in the mountains as he had done in the T/W [Tan War]', Johnny Connor in *The Men Will Talk to Me*, p. 255.

35   Abbott, *Police Casualties*, pp 315–32. Abbott offers a figure of 441 for the number of members of the Crown Forces killed in the three years of 1919–21.

36   Ibid., pp. 315–39 from 1 June 1921 to 11 July 1921.

37   Henry Bowles, Royal Irish Constabulary Service Records 1816–1922, British National Archives.

38   William Harvie, Royal Irish Constabulary Service Records 1816–1922, British National Archives.

39   Letter from 6th Battalion, Kerry No. 2 Brigade to Daniel Mulvihill, Papers of Daniel Mulvihill, (IE UCD/P64), UCD Archives.

40   Billy Mullins in *The Men Will Talk to Me*, p. 70.

41   Note on Joseph Duckett, Collins Papers, Military Archives.

42   Note on Daniel Lyons, Collins Papers, Military Archives.

43   Note on Daniel P. O'Shea, Collins Papers, Military Archives.

44   Tom O'Connor in *The Men Will Talk to Me*, p. 140. O'Connor does not name Constable Bergin in his account but he does refer to him as one of the police wounded at Ballymacandy (Bergin was shot in the leg) and that he was 'going with a girl here'. Bergin had been seeing a girl named Hixon from Milltown.

45 Herlihy, *Royal Irish Constabulary*, p. 137. McElligott established the Irish Branch of the National Union of Police and Prison Officers and also set up an organisation for resigned or dismissed RIC members.
46 RIC County Inspector's Report for June 1921.

Chapter Twelve

1 *Kerry People*, 4 June 1921.
2 *With the IRA in the Fight for Freedom*, p. 28.
3 Tom O'Connor in *The Men Will Talk to Me*, p. 138.
4 Pension application of John Heffernan.
5 Bertie Scully in *The Men Will Talk to Me*, p. 154.
6 Recollections of Dan Mulvihill, p. 11.
7 Murphy, *When Youth Was Mine*, p. 171.
8 Recollections of Dan Mulvihill, p. 11.
9 *Cork Examiner*, 28 June 1921.
10 Ernie O'Malley, *On Another Man's Wound* (Anvil Books, 1979), p. 336.
11 Horgan, *Dying for the Cause*, p. 249.
12 Con Casey memoirs; Horgan, *Dying for the Cause*, p. 263.
13 Horgan, *Dying for the Cause*, pp. 73–4.
14 Ibid.
15 Pension application of William Myles, father of Billy Myles, DP8427, Military Archives.
16 *Irish Press*, 2 June 1950 and *Cork Examiner*, 1 June 1950.
17 *Cork Examiner*, 1 June 1950.
18 O'Shea and Revington, *A Century of Politics in the Kingdom*, pp. 94–106.
19 Houlihan, *Cast a Laune Shadow*, p. 39. The IRA leader, Tom Barry was born in Killorglin in 1897 and led an ambush at Kilmichael, County Cork on 28 November 1920 which claimed the lives of up to sixteen Auxiliaries.
20 John O'Leary, *On the Doorsteps: Memoirs of a long-serving TD* (Irish Political Memoirs, 2015), pp 44–6; O'Shea and Revington, *A Century of Politics in the Kingdom*, pp. 51–61.
21 Recollections of Dan Mulvihill, p. 26.
22 O'Shea and Revington, *A Century of Politics in the Kingdom*, p. 61, p. 250.
23 *Freeman's Journal*, 8 September 1922.
24 *Kerry Reporter*, 21 June 1924.
25 *The Kerryman*, 5 January 1924.
26 Letter from Acting Command Adjutant to GHQ, 26 May 1924; Application from William Scully (father of Liam Scully), 1D270, Military Archives.
27 *The Kerryman*, 5 January 1924.
28 Letter from Acting Command Adjutant to GHQ, 26 May 1924; application from William Scully.
29 Letter from Major Leeson Marshall to his daughter, May, 12 June 1921; Leeson Marshall Papers, private collection.

30   Diary of Major Leeson Marshall, 20 June 1921.
31   Information courtesy of the Sheehan family.
32   Horgan, *Fighting for the Cause*, p. 258.
33   *The Kerryman*, 29 January 1972.

Chapter Thirteen

1   *Kerry People*, 4 June 1921.
2   www.theauxiliaries.com/men-alphabetical/men-m/mackinnon-ja/
     mackinnon.html retrieved 15 August 2019.
3   Pension application of Annie Cronin.
4   Letter from William M. Cahir & Co. Solicitors to the Secretary of the
     Department of Defence, 23 January 1985; pension application of Annie
     Cronin.
5   Guidance Note on Military Service Pensions Collection, www.
     militaryarchives.ie.
6   Guide to the Military Service (1916–1923) Pensions Collection
     (Department of Defence, 2012), Military Archives, p. 84.
7   Recollections of Dan Mulvihill, p. 26.
8   Guide to Military Pensions Collection, p. 71.
9   Introduction by Minister for Defence, Alan Shatter TD, in Guide to
     Military Service Pensions Collection, p. 9.
10   Pension application of Katie Mulvihill.
11   Letter from Dan Mulvihill, 21 March 1981, pension application of Katie
     Mulvihill.
12   I am grateful to Seán Breen for sharing the medal and pension application
     files of his grandfather, James Breen.
13   Letter from Thomas O'Connor, dated 24 May 1940 in support of application
     of Nora Corcoran; pension application of Nora Corcoran.
14   Pension application of Nora Corcoran.
15   Pension applications of Nora Corcoran and Nellie Foley.
16   Ibid.
17   Note on pension application file of Nellie Foley, dated 11 March 1941.
18   Gospel of Luke, 10:38–42, otherwise known as the story of Jesus at the
     home of Martha and Mary.
19   Guide to Military Pensions Collection, p. 135.
20   Letter from Thomas O'Connor to Department of Defence, undated;
     pension application of Thomas O'Connor, MP/34/REF4798.
21   *The Men Will Talk to Me*, p. 131.
22   Pension application of Mary [O'] Riordan (*née* Casey), MSP/34/REF62133,
     Military Archives.
23   Application from Maurice Cascy (Snr), 1D158, Military Archives.
24   Letter from Garda Edward Nagle, 16 May 1924; application from Maurice
     Casey (Snr).

25   Letter from Thomas Corcoran to Department of Defence, 16 November 1941, pension application of Thomas Corcoran.
26   Gavin Foster has found that Kerry No.1 and No.2 Brigade feature strongly in a cross-section of emigrants to Britain and the United States, *Atlas of the Irish Revolution*, pp. 741–7.
27   Letter from members of Keel Cumann na mBan to the Department of Defence, 24 March 1938; pension file of Nora Corcoran.
28   Horgan, *Fighting for the Cause*, pp. 92–6.
29   Ibid.
30   Footnote on Michael Duhig in Horgan, *Fighting for the Cause*, pp. 341–2.
31   Pension application of Edward Langford.
32   Foster, *Atlas of the Irish Revolution*, p. 747.
33   Information provided by John Knightly.
34   Liam Burke to Meriel Leeson Marshall, 19 December 1939, Leeson Marshall Papers, private collection.
35   Hannah Sugrue, Milltown to May Ruth, 11 December 1939, Leeson Marshall Papers, private collection.
36   O'Sullivan, *Irish Constabularies*, p. 379.
37   Information from Harry O'Neill.
38   BMH, WS 1,413, Tadhg Kennedy (appendices).
39   *Evening Echo*, 14 October 1921.
40   O'Halpin and Ó Corráin, *The Dead of the Irish Revolution*, pp. 455–6, 467.
41   *Irish Independent*, 17 November 1971.
42   *Limerick Leader*, 17 November 1971.
43   Information courtesy of Harry and Mary O'Neill.
44   Information provided to the author.

Postscript

1   'Milltowner', *The Kerryman*, 5 June 1971.
2   Recollections of Dan Mulvihill, p. 28.
3   *The Kerryman*, 3 April 1965.
4   Recollections of Dan Mulvihill, p. 24.
5   *The Kerryman*, 18 January 1985. Picture courtesy of Shane Mulvihill.
6   Letter from Dan Mulvihill to Timothy 'Chub' O'Connor TD, 5 December 1979 on file of pension application from Daniel Mulvihill, MSP/34/REF4800, Military Archives.
7   Charles Townshend, 'The Irish War of Independence: Context and Meaning' in Guide to the Military Service Pensions Collection, p. 110.

Appendices

1   'Milltown District Council, 6th Battalion, Kerry No.2 Brigade,' MA/MSPC/CMB/121, Military Archives.

INDEX

Abbeydorney RIC Barracks 80
Aiken, Frank 185
Allman, Daniel (Dan) 29, 34, 54, 55, 62, 69
Allman, May 34
Allman, Patrick (Pat) 29, 34, 165
Anglo-Irish Treaty 77, 159, 163
Anglo-Irish War *see* War of Independence
Army Pensions Acts 169, 175
Ashe, Gregory 57, 91
Ashe, Thomas 69
Atlas of the Irish Revolution 50
Auxiliary Division of the RIC (ADRIC) 19, 20–2, 23, 59; arrival in Dublin 22; fatalities 70, 71, 81; formation 21; IRA and 49; in Kerry 21–2; reign of terror 21; uniform 21

Ballybunion RIC Barracks 85
Ballykissane 70; drownings 13
Ballymacandy Ambush 8, 14–15, 63, 92–3, 100–9; aftermath 108–9, 113–14, 116–17, 149, 164; ambush participants (IRA) 157–60; arms, IRA and 101–2; Cahill's men and 79–80; casualties/fatalities 104, 106–8, 113–14, 120; first-hand accounts of 105–6; IRA casualty 142; map of area 10–11; Military Archives, list of those present 158; money taken from deceased 108, 150; newspaper coverage 140–2; plans/preparation for 101; police authorities' reaction to 153; reports on 123–4, 153–4; reprisals, absence of 144, 145–6, 147; scouts 93, 94, 95, 99–100, 101, 109, 175–6, 180; survivors 105, 110, 151–2, 182–3; tales/reminiscences of 182–3, 184; tip-off given to Black and Tans 95, 153; visit by surviving Black and Tan 182–3, 184; weapons taken by IRA 108; *see also* Military Court of Inquiry
Ballymullen Barracks 127, 128–9
Barrett, Timothy 89
Barry, Kevin 63
Barry, Thomas (RIC) 81
Barry, Thomas (Tom) 81
Battle of Ballyeagh (1834) 25
Beál na mBláth 29
Beard, Frederick J. (RIC Constable) 85, 151
Béaslaí, Piaras 20
Benson, Francis (RIC Head Constable) 70
Bergin, Patrick (RIC Constable): arms supplied to IRA 152, 153; Ballymacandy Ambush 106–7; emigration to Canada 152; family background 85; injuries 124, 125; IRA informer 152, 153
Black and Tans 19–20, 22, 23, 82; arrest of Dr Sheehan 165; arson

attacks 62, 77, 140; compensation for rampage 58; cycle patrol 82–3, 89, 93–4, 95; ex-servicemen in 19, 82, 83, 85–6; IRA attacks 32–3, 49, 54–6, 61–2, 70, 85; perception of 20, 22, 152; raids 35, 60; recruitment 19; reprisals 57–8, 59, 60; Siege of Tralee 77; uniform 19

Blake (RIC Head Constable) 68, 125

Boolteens 35, 74, 75, 91, 93, 149

Boolteens RIC Barracks 35, 44, 84

Borgonovo, John 53–4

Bowles, Henry Frederick (RIC Constable) 84–5, 106; injuries 124, 125, 151

Bowles, Henry Thomas 84–5

Brackhill 25, 78–9, 93; IRA and 30–1, 54

Brannock, Patrick (RIC Constable) 47

Breen, James 100, 171–2

Brosnan, Tadhg 90, 150; Ballymacandy Ambush 91, 103, 104; death 176; emigration 176; hideout (The Hut), based at 69, 74

Browne, John 158

Buckley, Revd Patrick 59, 118

Budd, Edgar (RIC Constable) 70–1

Bureau of Military History 105, 170, 179

Burke, William (Willie) 94

Cahill, Denis (RIC Constable) 124

Cahill, Mary and Thady 72

Cahill, Patrick J. (Paddy), TD 69, 72–3, 76–7, 149; anti-Treaty comrades 150; Cahill's men 79–80; cinema run by 77, 79; dispersal of men ordered by 150; elected to Dáil Éireann 77, 160; Flying Column, leadership of 74, 78, 88, 159; hideout (The Hut) and 73, 74, 75–6, 90–1; ill health 78, 90; *Kerry Champion* newspaper set up

by 161; loyalty to 79; Mulvihill's messages to 90; perception of 90; stood down as Officer Commanding 77–8, 79, 90

Callinafercy 38

Callinafercy House 40, 42, 43, 44, 110, 177

Callinafercy IRA 35, 54, 55, 70, 100, 155–6

Callinafercy National School 6

Callinafercy Volunteers 43

Carey, Major J.L.R. 129

Carroll, John 180

Caseley, Albert (RIC Constable) 56, 57, 58, 71, 86

Casey, John 87

Casey, Maurice (Mossie) 88, 158–9, 175

Casey, Maurice, Snr 175

Casey, Michael 88, 99, 104, 109

Casey, Nurse 142

Castledrum National School 35, 174

Castlegregory IRA 69, 74, 75, 79, 80, 91, 150, 176

Castlemaine 10–11; drownings 13; Griffin's Bar 95, 97, 99

Cathair Con Rí 72

Chambers, Captain C.S. 129, 136

Civil War 25, 162; anti-Treaty side 79, 150, 158, 159, 161, 162; Cumann na mBan and 172–3

civil-rights movement (Six Counties) 184–5

Clan na Gael 176

Clann na Poblachta 161

Cloghane Ambush 79

Clonmore Cottage 11, 101, 102, 103

Clúbháin, Biddy (Clifford) 86–7

Coffey, John 142

Collery, Anne 17

Collery, Anne (*née* O'Gara) 16

Collery, Catherine (*née* Collins) 17, 122; burial in Killagha Abbey

180; children 119, 126, 179, 181; compensation award 179; death 180; death of husband 119, 120, 125–6; deaths of children 179; departure from Milltown 178–9

Collery, James Christopher (RIC Sergeant) **10**, 16, 47; Ballymacandy Ambush 103–4, 108, 113; children 17, 119, 126, 179, 181; cycle patrol 83; death 104, 108, 113, 136, 143; family background 16; funeral 143, 155; Killorglin, relocation to 50, 68; marriage 17; memorial plaque, National Memorial Arboretum 180–1; Military Court of Inquiry 128–9, 130; Milltown, assignment to 17; promotion to sergeant 17; removal of remains to church 121, 148; residence 10, 18; RIC career 16–18; Taylor's arrest 118; War of Independence and 18

Collery, Revd James 179, 180

Collery, Michael 16

Collery, Patrick 16

Collery, Rita (Margaret Frances) 179, 181

Collins, Michael: death 29; Papers in the Military Archives 152

Connor, Johnny 76, 90, 161

Conscription Crisis 14, 26

Coogan, Eamon (Ned) 149

Cooney, Andy 79

Cooney, Joseph (RIC Constable) 68, 84; Ballymacandy Ambush 106–7, 108, 114, 118; compensation awarded to family 180; Military Court of Inquiry 128–9, 131; remains removed by train 125; removal of remains to church 121; Taylor's death and 118–19, 163

Corcoran, Cornelius 41

Corcoran, Nellie 34

Corcoran, Nora 35–6, 91, 92, 142; death 174; dressing station 172–3; military service pension claim 172, 173–4

Corcoran, Thomas 109, 173–4

Cork Examiner 56, 158, 160

Cosgrave, Liam (W.T.) 178

Coulter, Robert (Special Constable) 71

Courtney, Delia (*later* O'Connor) 174

Creaghe-Howard, Captain 40

Cromwell, Oliver 20, 61

Cronin, Annie J.: Civil War activities 167; Cuman na mBan and 34, 117, 144, 145; death 169; military service pension claim 167–9, 170; old age pension and 169

Cronin, Daniel 30

Cronin, James (Jimmy) 30, 44, 54, 67, 68; Ballymacandy Ambush 89, 103, 104, 117; Cahill, views on 90; hunger strike 167

Cronin, John 30, 168, 169

Cronin, Michael 98–9, 102–3

Cumann na mBan 24, 30, 80; activities 34–5; Ballymacandy Ambush casualties and 117, 142; Civil War, dressing station 172–3; emigration of members 176; Fries Company 88; food supplies, IRA and 76, 91–2; IRA and 33, 34–6, 54, 88; Keel Company 34–5, 36, 91, 142; in Kerry 33–4; member courtmartialled 59–60; membership in Kerry 33; military service pension claims 167–9, 170–1, 172, 173–4, 175; Milltown District Council 33–4; raids on houses 60; safe houses provided by 92, 142, 172; War of Independence and 33

Curtin, John (RIC Constable) 47

Dáil Éireann 14, 40, 77
Daly, Bernard 100
Daly, Charlie 49
Daly, James (Jimmy) 91
Daly, Jeremiah 94
Daly, Thomas (Tom) 49
de Valera, Éamonn 64, 155, 185
Dingle Peninsula 63, 72–4, 75, 108
Donoghue, Florrie 78–9
Dowd, Denis 30
Dowd, Mary 36, 76
Dublin Castle 96–7, 153
Duckett, Joseph 95–6
Duggan, Mary Ann (née Dowd) 35, 76
Duhig, Michael 91, 176

Eager, Nora (Nanno) (later O'Donovan Rossa) 38
Easter Rising (1916) 13, 25, 80
emigration 15, 16, 152, 174, 176–7
Evans, John Herbert (RIC Constable) 56, 57, 58, 71, 86
Evening Echo 124, 143

Famine 15, 38
Farmers' Bridge Company 49, 76, 90
Farson, Enid Eveleen (née Stoker) 32
Farson, Negley 32; Way Of A Transgressor, The 32
Fenian Rising 15, 38, 115
Ferriter, Diarmaid 4, 174
Ferriter, Pierce 116
Fianna Éireann, Na 79, 80, 89, 99, 157, 171; Castlemaine sluadh 99–100; military service pension claims 171; sluagh (branches) in Kerry 99, 171–2
Fianna Fáil 161, 185
Firies Cumann na mBan 88
Firies IRA 28, 64
First World War 19, 39, 40, 56, 82, 122
Fitzgerald, Maurice 69

Fitzgerald, Paddy Paul 79, 102, 103, 159–60
Fleming, Michael 80
Flynn, Edward 30
Flynn, James 30, 94
Flynn, John (Jack) 89, 90, 93; anti-Treaty stance 161; Ballymacandy Ambush 94; elected to Dáil 161; IRA and 11, 30, 54, 68; political career 30, 161–2
Flynn, Patrick 41
Foley, Archdeacon 146
Foley, Jerry 142
Foley, Nellie (née Corcoran) 35, 91–2, 142; death 174; dressing station 172–3; military service pension claim 172, 173–4
Foley, Patrick (RIC Constable) 55–7, 86, 95, 106, 151
Foley's garage 58
Fort Agnes (Poll na Ratha) 61, 71
Free State forces 159, 165
Freeman's Journal 162
Fybough hideout (The Hut) 73–6, 176; abandonment of 150; Cahill's men at 79–80, 102; food supplies 76, 91

GAA (Gaelic Athletic Association) 160
Gaelic League 58, 66
Gallagher, Edward 92
Galvin, Michael (Mick) 88–9, 90, 101
Galvin, Moss 90
Garvey, Patrick 75
General Election (1918) 14
General Election (1921) 77
German Plot 28, 80
Gilheany, Patrick (RIC Constable) 129
Glen Ellen 49, 116, 137
Glenbeigh railway station 69, 88
Glenbeigh RIC Barracks 49–50
Glencar IRA 20, 64, 82, 142, 156; ambush planned by 67–8;

attack on barracks 50; Killorglin residents, views on 66; Taylor, fatal shooting of 67–8; training 54

Glencar RIC Barracks 52, 68, 84

Godfrey demesne 39, 110, 162; Black Gate 117–18; gate lodge 112; sale of estate to tenantry 42

Godfrey family 18, 39, 40, 42, 43, 116

Godfrey, Helen 122

Godfrey, Sir John Fermor 43, 122

Godfrey, Lady Mary 42, 59, 119–20

Godfrey, Mabel (*later* Leeson Marshall) 43

Godfrey, Thomas 40

Godfrey, Sir William Cecil 42, 43, 59, 112

Gordon, Lady Edith, *Winds of Time, The* 43

Gortatlea RIC Barracks 14, 99

Greenwood, Sir Hamar 56

Griffin's Bar, Castlemaine 95, 97, 99

Hall, James (Special Constable) 71

Hamilton (RIC District Inspector) 123, 124

Hanafin, Edward (Eddie) 100, 157, 158

Hanafin, Irene (*later* Sheehan) 116

Hanafin, Jack 157

Hanafin, James 48, 116

Hargrave, Abraham Addison 127–8, 130–1, 132–3; Military Court of Inquiry testimony 134–5

Harrington, Edward 38–9

Harvie, William (RIC Constable) 84, 97; ambush tip-off 95; Ballymacandy Ambush 105–6; injuries 124, 125, 151; Military Court of Inquiry 130; pension/compensation awarded to 151

Haughey, Charles J. 186

Hawley, Tommy 69

Headford Junction Ambush 29, 69

Healy, Daniel 29, 54

Healy, Denis (school principal) 6

Healy, Kathy 34

Hearn, James (RIC Constable) 85, 151

Heffernan, John P. (Jack Captain) 33, 35, 55, 100, 112

Herlihy, Jim (RIC historian) 16

Hillville Ambush 54–5, 58, 60, 63, 86; reprisals 57–8, 59, 60, 144

Hobson, Bulmer 99

Hogan, Eugene 80, 102

Holmes, Philip Armstrong (RIC Divisional Commissioner) 145

Home Rule 27, 40, 43, 44

Home Rule Bill 39

Horan, Ned 64

Horgan, Tim 149, 158, 176; *Fighting for the Cause* 176

Houlihan, Patrick 161

Howlett, George (RIC Constable) 145

Hurley, James (Jim) 29–30

informers 70, 76, 95–6

intimidation: hair cropping 50–1; of Protestant community 41; tarring 50–1, 55

Irish Independent 57; Ballymacandy Ambush 140–1; funeral of Constable McCormack 143

Irish National Boy Scouts *see* Fianna Éireann, Na

Irish Parliamentary Party 14, 66, 115

Irish Press 160

Irish Republican Army (IRA) 6, 14, 18; 1st Southern Division 27–8; 2nd Battalion, Kerry No.2 Brigade 28; 3rd Cork Brigade 29; 4th Battalion, Kerry No.2 Brigade 28; 4th Castlegregory Battalion 91; 6th Battalion, Kerry No.2 Brigade 28, 67, 76; 9th Battalion 79, 159; Active Service Units 53; ambushes 31, 32, 54–5, 61–2, 69, 70, 79, 81; ammunition, shortage

of 88; assassinations 48, 70; Beál
na mBláth ambush 29; Black and
Tans and 60–1, 70; civilian fatality
110; Cork No.2 Brigade 70, 109;
Cumann na mBan and 33, 34–6,
54, 88; Farmers' Bridge Company
49; fatalities 67, 69; First Southern
Division 78, 150; Flying Columns
29, 53–4, 69, 73–4, 78, 88; food
supplies, Cumann na mBan and
76, 91–2; homemade explosives
158–9; informers 70, 76, 95–6;
Kerry No.1 Brigade 28, 49, 57, 73,
77–8, 91, 171; Kerry No.2 Brigade
28, 29, 70; Kerry No.3 Brigade
28, 69–70, 72; plans for assaults
156; raiding/road-trenching/mail
robbery 64–6; ranks, expansion
of 155–6; retreat to Keel 63; RIC
and 18–19, 45–6, 49–50, 67–8;
road-trenching 49, 64–5, 82–3, 87;
safe houses 30, 74, 92, 172; scouts
93, 94, 95, 99, 157, 171–2; tactics
31, 32; tarring 55; Truce, reaction
to 156–7; weapons, lack of 64;
weapons seized by 69; see also
Fybough hideout (The Hut)
Irish Republican Brotherhood (IRB)
25, 38, 80, 99
Irish Times, Ballymacandy Ambush
141–2
Irish Volunteers 18, 26;
Ballymacelligott Company 14;
drownings 13; in Kerry 27, 39;
Milltown Company 29, 39
Irregulars 162, 163

Jeffers, Daniel (Dan) 79–80
John Mitchels GAA Club 160
Joy, Sinéad 15, 64, 78

Kautt, W.H. 101
Keane, Daniel 41

Keane, Fergal 20, 22
Keane, William (Billy) 99, 100
Keating, Con 13
Keating, Daniel (Dan) 90, 95
Keel Cumann na mBan 91, 176
Keel House 74, 149
Keel IRA 31, 36, 63, 69, 89
Kerry Champion 161
Kerry People 50, 64, 147; arson 146;
Ballymacandy Ambush 135–6;
peace talks 155
Kerryman, The 37, 125; 'Milltown
Notes' 37; 'Milltowner'
contributions 184; offices/printing
presses burned 140
Kerrymen's Irish Republican Club 176
Kilburn House, training camp at 167
Kilcoleman Abbey **10**, 18, 40, 42, 59
Kilderry Wood Ambush 61, 62, 63, 92
Kildysart RIC Barracks 71
Kilflynn 62
Kilgarvan RIC Barracks 49
Killagha Abbey (Abbey of Our Lady
of Bello Loco) 10, 61, 180
Killarney Echo and South Kerry
Chronicle 39, 41, 49; the Irish
Pariah 22–3
Killorglin: attack on creamery 62;
IRA activity 66; Irish Volunteers,
attitude to 66
Killorglin Boy Scouts 39
Killorglin IRA 55
Killorglin RIC Barracks 50, 55–6, 66,
67, 68, 71, 81, 129; IRA plans to
attack 156; policemen stationed
at 83–5
Kilmichael Ambush 81
Kiltallagh IRA 60, 94, 159
King, Alice Mary 110
King, Kate 110, 120
King, Captain William Herbert 110
King, Revd William John 110, 111,
148

Knightly, John 42
Knightly, Thomas 94

Lady Wicklow, SS 159
Lambe, James (school principal) 6
land reform 62
Land War 15, 38
Langford, Edward (Ned) 55, 70, 177
Leary, Timothy 94
Leeson, David M. 20
Leeson Marshall, Mabel (*née* Godfrey)
    43–4
Leeson Marshall, Major Markham
    Richard 42–3, 58, 59, 110, 177–8;
    Ballymacandy Ambush 110–11,
    125–6, 147–8; Constable Collery's
    funeral 143; Constable Quirke,
    perception of 84; daughter's
    wedding 177; death 178; Fr
    O'Sullivan, perception of 143,
    148; IRA letter to 146; letter
    to daughter 147–8, 164; road
    conditions, IRA and 65, 134
Leeson Marshall, Mary 42
Leeson Marshall, May 44; letter from
    father 147–8, 164
Leeson Marshall, Meriel (*née* Hodson)
    44, 65, 110, 125, 148
Lispole Ambush 69
Lispole IRA 57
Listowel RIC Barracks 46
Listry Company 28–9, 54, 62
Listry Creamery 62
Lixnaw 62
Lloyd George, David 47, 56–7, 155
Lucey, Con 54
Lynch, Fionán, TD 35, 91
Lynch, James (RIC Constable) 47
Lynch, Liam 78–9, 150

McCarthy, Cornelius (RIC Constable)
    47
McCarthy (RIC Sergeant) 75

McCarthy, Richard 99–100
McCaughey, Michael Francis
    (RIC District Inspector) 81–2;
    Ballymacandy Ambush 103, 104,
    105, 108, 113–14; Black and Tans,
    member of 82; compensation
    awarded to widow 179; cycle
    patrol 82–3, 93–4, 95, 96–7; death
    104, 108, 113; First World War
    and 82; Griffin's Bar, Castlemaine
    95, 97, 99; Irish Guards and 82;
    Military Court of Inquiry 128–9,
    130; remains removed by train
    125; removal of remains to church
    121; Royal Irish Rifles and 82; tip-
    off given to 95, 96, 100, 130, 154
Mac Coluim, Fionán 57–8
Mac Conmara, Tomás 22
McCormack, John Stratton (RIC
    Constable) 97; Ballymacandy
    Ambush 104, 108, 114;
    compensation awarded to
    family 180; death 128, 133, 148,
    150–1; family background 83, 128;
    funeral 143–4; injuries 120–1,
    122–3, 124; medical treatment
    120–1, 122–3, 124, 132–3;
    Military Court of Inquiry 128–9,
    131–4, 136; moved by train 125
McElligott, Thomas (RIC Constable)
    152
McEllistrim, Thomas (Tom), TD 168,
    171, 172
McGill, Henry (RIC Head Constable)
    129–30
McGillycuddy of the Reeks 32
McKenna, Pat (local historian) 18, 122
Mackinnon, Agnes Beatrice 166–7,
    178, 179
Mackinnon, Lt John Alistair 22, 59,
    76; assassination 76, 127, 166
McLoughlin, Thomas 94, 159
McMahon, Michael (Forker) 79

MacSwiney, Terence 63
Maguire, Joseph (RIC Constable) 70
Malcolm, Elizabeth 16
Marconi House, London 26
Marconi School of Wireless, London 25
Markievicz, Constance, Countess 99
Mason, Alexander (Sonny) 60, 94, 104, 109, 171
Mason, Amelia 60, 171
Mason, James 100
Mason, Oliver 94, 109–10
Mee, Jeremiah (RIC Constable) 46
Military Archives 157; IRA Brigade Reports 158; Michael Collins Papers 152; military pensions applications 169, 174
Military Court of Inquiry 127–39; conclusion: 'guilty of wilful murder' 136; conflict of evidence 134, 136; disciplinary measures, Sheehan and 137–9; Hargrave's testimony 134–5; O'Halloran's testimony 132–3; Sheehan's actions, assessment of 136–8, 164–5; Sheehan's testimony 133–4, 136–7; telephone numbers listed for Milltown 137; Whinton's testimony 133, 134, 137
military service pensions: Advisory Committee 169–70; Board of Assessors 169, 170, 171; Cumann na mBan applications 167–9, 170–3, 175; Fianna Éireann applications 171–2
Military Service Pensions Acts 169
Milltown 10, 37–9; arson, threat of 60–1; police curfew 50; Protestant community, intimidation of 41; shops/businesses 98; Sinn Féin club 26; Spout, the (community focal point) 87; telephone numbers, unlisted 137
Milltown Company 29, 39, 90

Milltown RIC Barracks 23, 44; arson attempt 31–2; cleaner (Biddy the Barracks) 86–7; Collery and 17, 23; communications equipment 49; IRA attack 49; relocation to new headquarters 48–9; Smyth (Divisional Commissioner), instructions issued by 45–6, 47
Milltown School (The Little Academy) 5
Milltown Tenants' Association 40
Monahan, Charles 13
Moore, Martin 14
Moran, Timothy (RIC Constable) 129
Moriarty, Daniel 99
Moyderwell 80
Moyderwell Technical School, Tralee 22
Moylan, Seán 109
Mullins, William (Billy) 19, 57, 73, 79, 80, 151
Mulvihill, Cornelius 25
Mulvihill, Daniel (Dan) 11, 24–5, 125; Advisory Committee, military service pensions 169–70; agricultural studies in Clonakilty 27, 29; ammunition 88; Ballymacandy Ambush 101, 102, 107–8, 158; Ballymacandy site, assessment of 93; Black and Tan survivor, attitude towards 183, 184; Black and Tans cycle patrol 89–90; Board of Assessors, military service pensions 170; civil-rights movement, views on 185; Cumann na mBan and 34–5; death 186; family background 24–5; family farm, sale of 174; Fianna Fáil and 185; Flynn, support for 161–2; Glencar, withdrawal to 52–3; IRA and 24, 29, 52–4, 61, 68; IRA meeting at Brackhill 78–9; Kerry, descriptions

of 53; Killorglin RIC, attack on
68–9; letter to Timothy (Chub)
O'Connor 186; Milltown Barracks,
attack on 31–2, 49; Milltown
IRA 29; radio operator career 26;
republicanism and 27; Royal Air
Force, interest in 26; Saor Éire
membership 185; Sinn Féin club
and 26; Spike Island, flag raising
at 185; studies in London 25;
Truce, reaction to 157
Mulvihill, Katie 88, 109; death 171;
military service pension claim
170–1
Mulvihill, Nora 24–5
Mulvihill, Patrick 26–7, 29
Murphy, Humphrey (Free) 78
Murphy, Jeremiah 14, 144, 156–7
Murphy, Paddy 67
Myles, Billy 75, 80, 160
Myles, Jerry 80; Ballymacandy
Ambush 102, 107, 116, 117, 142,
149; funeral, Old IRA guard of
honour 160; injuries/recuperation
107, 142–3, 160; obituary 160
Myles, Molly 80

Nagle, Edward (Garda) 175
Nagle, George 100
National Memorial Arboretum,
Staffordshire 180–1
Nolan, Revd J. 143–4
Noraid 176
Northern Ireland, civil-rights
movement 184–5

O'Brien, Bryan (Bryannie) 36, 92,
107–8, 175–6
O'Brien, John 94
O'Brien, Mary 142
Ó Ceallaigh, Seán T. 115
O'Connell, Daniel, Repeal Campaign
38

O'Connell, Daniel (architect) 122
O'Connor, Revd Batt 5, 38
O'Connor, Jeremiah (Jerry) (Unkey)
80, 102, 103–4
O'Connor, Thomas 80, 101–2
O'Connor, Thomas (Tom) 28, 40–1,
59, 60–1, 66, 89, 90; Ballymacandy
Ambush 94, 101, 102, 103, 104,
109; Civil War injuries 172–3;
emigration to North America
174; hideout (The Hut) and 76;
imprisonment 28; Killorglin RIC,
attack on 68–9; Leeson Marshall,
letter to 146; marriage 174–5;
military service pension claim
174, 175; plans for assaults 156;
Rae's arrest 149; RIC sergeant and
75; weapons seized by 69
O'Connor, Timothy (Chub), TD 168,
169, 185; Mulvihill's letter to 186
O'Donnell, Peadar 185
O'Donnell, Thomas (Tom), MP 39,
44, 66
O'Donoghue, Donnchadha 80
O'Donoghue, Revd M. 144
O'Donovan, Dinny 58
O'Donovan Rossa, Jeremiah 38
O'Halloran, M.H. 131–2
Old IRA veterans 168, 184, 185
O'Leary, Michael 75, 79, 103, 150, 171
O'Leary, Timothy 99
O'Malley, Ernie 158
O'Neill, Thomas P. (Tip) 1
O'Shea, Jack 59
O'Shea, Maggie 18
O'Shea, Maria 76
O'Shee, John Marcus Poer (RIC
County Inspector) 47, 48
Ó Siochfhradha, Pádraig (An Seabhac)
36
O'Sullivan, Revd Alexander (Sandy)
59–60, 67, 117–19; Ballymacandy
Ambush casualties and

118–19, 123, 135–6; Free State
government, support for 163;
funeral of Constable Collery 143,
181; IRA and 162–3; perception
of 143, 148; remains of deceased
121–2; shots fired at 162–3
O'Sullivan, Daniel (Big Dan) 80
O'Sullivan, D.M. 57
O'Sullivan, Donal 15, 178
O'Sullivan, Eileen 114
O'Sullivan, John 80, 159–60
O'Sullivan, Mary (May) 36
O'Sullivan, Michael 94
O'Sullivan, Patrick V., *I Heard the
Wild Birds Sing* 44
O'Sullivan, Thomas (Totty) 7–8, 86–8,
117, 121
O'Toole, Peter (RIC Constable) 47–8

Papal Army, Irish Battalion 115
Paulinus, Brother 5, 6–7, 88
Peamount Sanatorium, Dublin 160
Pearse, Pádraig 80
Perkins, Walter (RIC Constable) 71
Pius IX, Pope 115
Portmagee RIC Barracks 49
Pound Height 87
Power, George, Dean of Ardfert,
Rector of Killorglin 123, 126
Prendergast family 38
Presentation Brothers 5, 128
Presentation Convent School 17
Presentation Sisters 5
Protestant community, intimidation
of 41
Provisional IRA 176
Puck Fair 66–7
Purcell, Sister Xavier 17

Quirke, Denis 41, 68, 89, 168
Quirke, John (RIC Constable) 47, 84,
148; Ballymacandy Ambush 104,
108, 114; compensation awarded

to family 180; death 104, 108,
114; Military Court of Inquiry
128–9, 131; remains removed by
train 125; removal of remains to
church 121

Rae, Ellen 74, 150
Rae, Greta 74–5
Rae, Stephen (Steve) (IRA Intelligence
Officer) 74–5, 93, 149–50
Rae, William Emperor 74
Rathmore, Bog Road Ambush 70
Reilly, Edward (RIC Constable) 47
Restoration of Order in Ireland Act
(1920) 32
Rice, John Joe 162
Riordan, Mary (*née* Casey) 175
Roche, Brother Gonzaga 128
Rockfield 29, 34, 49, 54, 165
Rockfield National School 6
Rohan, Daniel (Dan) 91, 176
Royal Air Force (RAF) 26
Royal Irish Constabulary (RIC) 15–16;
attacks on barracks 14, 31, 44,
49–50; attacks on 41; closure of
barracks 49, 50; Commissioner
Smyth, instructions issued by
45–8; County Inspectors' reports
65; demonisation of 22–3; Dingle
Peninsula, report on 73; Dingle
Peninsula, round up plan 108;
District Inspectors, visits of 45;
Divisional Commissioner for
Munster 45–7; fatalities 18, 70–1,
79, 108, 145, 150–1; informers
for IRA 152; IRA and 18–19,
45–6, 49–50, 67–8; membership
15–16; nationalism and 152;
perception of RIC families 44–5;
police union, establishment of
162; public perception of 15;
reprisals 70, 71, 144–5; travel
patterns, ambushes and 90; War

of Independence and 18; widows
and children, hardship endured by
178–9; *see also* Auxiliary Division
of the RIC (ADRIC); Black and
Tans
Royal Munster Fusiliers 43, 128
Ryan, James 185

safe houses, IRA and 30, 74, 92, 172
Saor Éire 185
Scully, Michael 88, 104
Scully, Seán (Bertie) 20, 50, 66, 67,
68, 142; IRA companies 156;
Irregulars and 163; McCaughey,
views on 82; plans for assaults 156
Shanahan, Sister Theresa 17
Shea, Laurence 25
Shea, Pensioner 120–1, 122, 132;
cottage 10, 101, 102, 103, 117
Sheehan, Daniel Thomas (Dr
Dan) 11, 13, 34, 48–9, 114–16;
Ballymacandy Ambush casualties
116–17, 120, 122–3, 124, 136;
Black and Tans and 165; death
165; disciplinary measures,
possibility of 137–9; family
background 115; IRA medical
officer 116, 139; McCormack,
ambulance requested for 121,
123, 124, 133, 134; McCormack,
treatment of injuries 120, 122–3,
124, 131, 133–4; medical studies
115; Military Court of Inquiry's
assessment of 136–8; residence
48–9, 116; testimony to Military
Court of Inquiry 133–4, 136–7
Sheehan, Eamon (Bunny) 165, 168
Sheehan, Irene (*née* Hanafin) 116, 165
Sheehan, Jeremiah Daniel 115
Sheehan, William 20
Siege of Tralee 63, 77
Sinn Féin 66; abstentionist stance 77,
162; General Election (1918) 14;

General Election (1921) 77
Sinn Féin club, Milltown 26
Slattery, Con 59
Slattery, J. 100
Slattery, Margaret 34, 59–60
Smyth, Gerald Bryce Ferguson (RIC
Divisional Commissioner):
assassination of 48; instructions
issued by 45–8
Snoxell, Lieutenant Frank 123–4
Soloheadbeg, County Tipperary 14
Spike Island, Cork 185
Stack, Austin 35, 76, 161
Stephens, Charles 110, 111
Stephens, James 121
Stephens' Mill 58
Stoker, George 32
Storey, William (RIC Head Constable)
70
Sugrue, Denis 7–8, 37, 44–5, 117, 121,
184
Sugrue, Hannah 178
Sugrue, Joseph (Joe) 80
Sullivan, Patrick 100
Sullivan, Thomas 70
Synge, J.M., *Playboy of the Western
World, The* 115

Tan War *see* War of Independence
Taylor, Joseph (Joe) 82, 84, 85, 163;
Constable Cooney and 118; fatal
wounding of 67–8, 108; gun 108
tenant activism 40, 41–2
Times, The, Ballymacandy Ambush
142
Townshend, Charles 4, 187
Tralee: Fianna Éireann branch 99;
Irish Republican Brotherhood 80;
Siege of 63, 77; Volunteers 80
Tralee Military Hospital 132
Tralee Quarter Sessions 166–7, 179
Tralee Urban District Council 79, 80,
160

Truce 150, 156–7, 165
Tudor, General H.H. 166
Twomey, William J. (RIC Constable)
    85, 151

Victoria, Queen 15

War of Independence 6, 42, 81;
    Cumann na mBan and 33; in
    Kerry 13–15; legacy of 187;
    Milltown and 7; peace talks 155;
    RIC and 18
Watson's Creamery 62
Whelan, William (Billy) 161

Whinton, Ellen 119–20
Whinton, William (ex-RIC Sergeant)
    44, 112–15, 119, 126; ambulance
    requested by 134; Ballymacandy
    Ambush 113–14, 116, 120;
    McCormack helped by 122–3,
    132, 133; Military Court of
    Inquiry, testimony 133, 134, 137;
    perception of 112
Willis, Colonel Commandant E.H.
    129
Wilson, Field Marshal Henry 19
Wilson, Lieutenant M. 129
Wyndham Land Act (1903) 42

Printed in Great Britain
by Amazon